M3 MEDIUM TANK
vs
PANZER III

Kasserine Pass 1943

GORDON L ROTTMAN

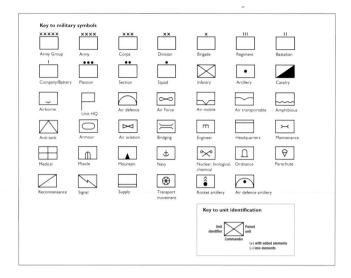

Key to military symbols

Army Group	Army	Corps	Division	Brigade	Regiment	Battalion
Company/Battery	Platoon	Section	Squad	Infantry	Artillery	Cavalry
Airborne	Unit HQ	Air defence	Air Force	Air mobile	Air transportable	Amphibious
Anti-tank	Armour	Air aviation	Bridging	Engineer	Headquarters	Maintenance
Medical	Missile	Mountain	Navy	Nuclear, biological, chemical	Ordnance	Parachute
Reconnaissance	Signal	Supply	Transport movement	Rocket artillery	Air defence artillery	

Key to unit identification

Unit identifier — Parent unit
Commander
(+) with added elements
(−) less elements

First published in Great Britain in 2008 by Osprey Publishing,
Midland House, West Way, Botley, Oxford OX2 0PH, UK
443 Park Avenue South, New York, NY 10016, USA

E-mail: info@ospreypublishing.com

© 2008 Osprey Publishing Ltd.

A CIP catalog record for this book is available from the British Library

ISBN: 978 1 84603 261 5

Page layout by: Ken Vail Graphic Design
Index by Alan Thatcher
Typeset in ITC Conduit and Adobe Garamond
Maps by Peter Bull Studio and The Map Studio
Originated by PDQ Digital Media Solutions
Printed in China through Bookbuilders

08 09 10 11 12   10 9 8 7 6 5 4 3 2 1

For a catalog of all books published by Osprey Military and Aviation please contact:

NORTH AMERICA
Osprey Direct, c/o Random House Distribution Center, 400 Hahn Road, Westminster, MD 21157

E-mail: info@ospreydirect.com

ALL OTHER REGIONS
Osprey Direct UK, P.O. Box 140 Wellingborough, Northants, NN8 2FA, UK

E-mail: info@ospreydirect.co.uk

www.ospreypublishing.com

Osprey Publishing is supporting the Woodland Trust, the UK's leading woodland conservation charity, by funding the dedication of trees.

Artist's note

Readers may care to note that the original painting from which the battlescene color plate in this book was prepared is available for private sale. All reproduction copyright whatsoever is retained by the Publishers. All inquiries should be addressed to:

Giuseppe Rava
Via Borgotto 17
48018 Faenza (RA)
ITALY

giuseppe.rava@fastnet.it

The Publishers regret that they can enter into no correspondence upon this matter.

CONTENTS

Introduction   4

Chronology   6

Design and Development   8

The Strategic Situation   22

Technical Specifications   31

The Combatants   41

Combat   57

Statistics and Analysis   73

Aftermath   75

Bibliography and Further Reading   78

Index   80

INTRODUCTION

The 1930s saw a great many advances in tank design by all major countries. Innovations included heavier and improved armor, larger caliber guns – with a reduction in machine guns, more powerful engines, higher speeds, longer range, and improved suspension systems that increased a tank's cross-country abilities. Yet there was still much to be learned, and the most valuable lessons had to be learned on the battlefield.

The war had no more than begun when a race evolved between the opposing sides to improve armor and install bigger guns on their tanks. Efforts were made to upgrade existing tanks, and to reduce the time necessary to field better tanks; models were redesigned and upgraded while still more improved models were undergoing design, testing, development, and production.

The US M3 medium tank, called the "Lee" and "Grant" by the British, was an example of this. It was based on the earlier M2 and was somewhat of a cobbled together design in order to put a 75mm gun on a tank in quick order. The rushed design suffered from numerous deficiencies, but it fulfilled a dire need, and thus the Grant and Lee saw service in the Western Desert in Africa with the British from May 1942. The M3 spawned the M4 Sherman medium tank, which was to later become the main Allied battle tank. Rife with flaws, the M3 had its strong points as well. Most, in American hands anyway, served on as training tanks by units not yet issued M4s. The M3 chassis also went on to become other vehicles ranging from tank recovery vehicles to self-propelled howitzers.

The Germans' most numerous tank was the PzKpfw III, the *Panzerkampfwagen* (armor battle vehicle), although what the British called the "Mk III" has since been overshadowed by the better known Tiger and Panther tanks. The *Panzer drei* (Panzer three), however, was by far the most numerous German light tank in Africa. It is often thought of as a medium tank because the machine gun-armed PzKpfw I and

PzKpfw II were usually called light tanks. The 7.5cm short gun-armed PzKpfw IV was the new medium infantry support tank. The PzKpfw III initially had a 3.7cm gun, but a short 5cm was soon introduced followed by a long 5cm, providing an effective antitank gun.

However, there is a lot more to tank warfare than just the tanks. Other critical aspects of tank warfare include tactics and logistics. The United States went to war with an unrealistic and incompletely developed doctrine, using more of a cavalry mindset of charging en masse. The Americans had studied and implemented lessons learned from combat in Europe and North Africa, but there were still many lessons they needed to learn, by performing under the stress and complexities of actual combat, in order to become lethal tankers. Although even in the early stage of the war, American logistics were far superior and richer than those of any other combatant, German veterans certainly had the edge on the Americans in regard to hard-won experience.

It is often said that the February 1943 Kasserine Pass battles[1] were the first engagements between green US troops and German Afrikakorps veterans. It may have been the first significant battle, but the first engagement was on November 25–26, 1942, at Chouigui Pass. This small engagement was between 1st Battalion, 1st Armored Regiment equipped with M3 light tanks and a platoon of halftrack-mounted 75mm howitzers (but lacking infantry, artillery, or engineers) and Panzer-Abteilung 190 elements with three or more PzKpfw IIIs with 5cm guns and at least six PzKpfw IVs with long 7.5cm guns. The 75mm howitzers fired first on the German tanks without effect but forced them to withdraw. One American tank company then attacked the German flank and lost six tanks within minutes, but another company maneuvered to attack the German rear, and with their 37mm guns knocked out six PzKpfw IVs and at least one PzKpfw III. These two companies then attacked an Italian infantry unit dismounting from trucks and largely destroyed it. While by no means a decisive engagement, the Americans were recognizing their tactical and equipment

A photograph of an early variation of the M2 tank which was the direct forerunner of the M3. (MHI)

inadequacies. However, they did not make adjustments quickly enough. Numerous other engagements were fought with the Germans prior to mid-February 1943, with the M3 mediums seeing action in late November and early December 1942. However, at this stage most of the US losses were due to antitank guns rather than by fire from German tanks.

The inexperienced Americans and veteran Germans would face one another in a more desperate battle in the early months of 1943 on the plains and hills of west-central Tunisia. In this ensuing duel both sides would learn much from one another and of themselves.

---

1 See Osprey Campaign 152, *Kasserine Pass 1943*.

CHRONOLOGY

1934
January — Requirement for PzKpfw III announced.

1937
May — First production of PzKpfw III.

1940
October — British purchasing commission signs contracts for US M3 light and medium tanks.

1941
March — M3 design completed.
April — M3 pilot models built.
October — M3 medium reclassified substitute standard when M4 was standardized.

1942
February — M3 light and medium tank delivered to the British.
May 26–June 18 — Combat debut of M3 mediums with UK during the Gazala Line battle.
October 23– — Battle of El Alamein, resulting in

The Germans tested several prototypes of PzKpfw III variants in efforts to improve the design. This is one of two 1939 Daimler-Benz Typ ZW40 tanks fitted with a diesel engine and the large interleafed road wheels as used on halftracks.

November 5 — Rommel's retreat toward Tunisia.
November 8 — Operation *Torch* commences with Allied landings in Morocco and Algeria.
November 11 — Vichy French forces sign armistice. Eighth Army enters Libya.
December 3 — After weeks of advancing into

A photograph showing a German Panzer III after it has been captured by British troops in North Africa. (IWM E 16567)

This overhead shot clearly shows the right-hand side sponson gun, turret, and turret machine-gun cupola which were distinctive features of the M3. (NARA)

Tunisia and Libya, German counterattacks regain some territory.

December 17	Germans commence withdrawal from Libya.
December 22	British commence attacks near Medjez el Bab.
December 24	Allied attacks in Tunisia are halted.

1943

January 14	21. Panzer-Division deployed to halt Allied advance from west.
January 15	British recommence offensive.
January 18	Tiger tanks are committed for the first time.
January 23	Tripoli falls to British.
January 25	US forces secure Maknassy.
January 30	21. Panzer-Division pushes back US and French units at Faïd.
February 14	10. and 21. Panzer-Divisionen attack II US Corps near Faïd, defeating US forces at Sidi Bou Zid.
February 15	German attack reinforced by elements of 15. Panzer-Division.
February 17	German attack continues with two-thirds of 1st US Armored Division destroyed.
February 19	Germans attack toward Kasserine Pass and Sbiba; both routes defended by US and British troops.
February 20	Germans seize Kasserine Pass and almost make it to Sbiba but are held by the British.
February 21–22	Battered British and US units halt German drives toward Thala, Tébasse, and Sbiba. US reinforcements help push Germans back, and Rommel commences a withdrawal.
February 24–26	Axis command is reorganized, and their forces continue to withdraw while conducting delaying attacks.
April	M3 medium reclassified limited standard as sufficient M4s become available.
May 12	Axis forces in Tunisia surrender.

1944

April	M3 medium declared obsolete.

DESIGN AND DEVELOPMENT

THE M3

The M2 medium tank of 1940 provided the basic design for the future M3 medium tank. Note the similar dual bogie wheels, steep glacis, centered driver's compartment, although it provided multiple large vision ports, and side escape hatches. The corner machine gun sponsons can be seen.

The US Army did not possess a medium tank in the 1930s, although several developmental designs existed on paper, and in some cases, prototypes were built through the 1920s. These exhibited British influence and bore small-caliber, low-velocity guns. In May 1936 the Army's Ordnance Committee directed the development of a new tank based on Infantry Board requirements.[2] Designated the T5, the projected medium tank was an enlarged M2 light tank, the predecessor of the M3 and M5 Stuarts. Some M2 components were used in the T5, but the new tank was to have heavier armor and armament. The T5's armament was little different from that on its light counterpart. It was envisioned as an infantry support tank and not for tank-to-tank combat.

The T5's chassis was not unlike the future M3's. The front glacis was well sloped, but the superstructure's sides and rear were vertical and further made vulnerable by numerous vision/pistol ports. The centerline driver's position had large shuttered ports to the front and sides.

---

2   A machine gun-armed M1 medium tank was standardized in April 1939, which had been built in 1936 as the T4. The 18 in service were declared obsolete a year later.

The high, boxy superstructure mounted a cramped centerline turret with the new 37mm M3 high-velocity gun. A .30cal machine gun in each of the four corner sponsons provided 360-degree defense. On either side of the turret and between the sponsons were manholes mounting a .30cal for antiaircraft, which had to be dismounted to allow the turret to traverse. Two fixed forward-firing machine guns were fitted in the glacis near the track guard fenders. It lacked a coaxial machine gun, but bristling with eight, that was not a real deficiency. The five-man crewed tank had a high profile, a characteristic that would plague US tanks for years. Its armor was comparatively heavy for the era, the lower front being 1.125in. and the vertical sides 1.25in.

Left front view of the M3 tank displaying its full armament. An M2 machine gun tripod is stowed aft of the headlight. This tank mounts the 75mm M5 short gun, which has not been fitted with a muzzle counterweight.

The 1937 T5 Phase 1 prototype was fitted with a wooden mock-up superstructure, and various armament arrangements were tested. The Phase 2 was a never-built concept study. The Phase 3, after trying out further armament arrangements, was standardized as the M2 medium tank in summer 1938. The T4E2 had only a machine gun turret and a much-modified glacis, with the driver's station moved to the left and a 75mm M1A1 pack howitzer mounted in the right front. This concept would be used in the M3.

With a major war in Europe, the first of 18 M2 medium tanks rolled out of the Rock Island Arsenal in Illinois in early 1940. The M2A1 was soon approved, featuring a redesigned turret, a more powerful engine, and other improvements. The first six already obsolete M2A1s were delivered in December 1940 and 88 more were delivered in 1941. Rock Island was incapable of producing sufficient numbers, and in August 1940, the Chrysler Motors Corporation was contracted for 1,000 M2A1s to be delivered by August 1942. The massive Detroit Tank Arsenal first had to be built by the US Army at Warren, Michigan, and would be operated by Chrysler.

The right front of an M3 tank. This one still has the two .30cal machine guns in the left glacis seen beside the headlight. Beside the right headlight can be seen the siren, meant to be a psychological weapon.

Battle reports from Poland told of the German PzKfz IV with a short 75mm gun employed for infantry support and the PzKfz III with a high-velocity 37mm. Both tanks had low profiles. In a rush to field something comparable, work began in the United States on what was hoped to be a formidable tank, the M3 medium. The German offensive into the Low Countries and France, coupled with the

9

This later M3A5 has the side escape hatches eliminated. Note the ventilator added behind the escape hatch aft of the main gun and the equipment stowage boxes on the glacis and over the driver's compartment. These were usually removed in combat. Note the return rollers are fitted to rearward extensions at the top of the bogie wheel suspension.

expanded use of the PzKfz IV, reinforced the need for a heavily armed US medium tank. Additionally, in late 1940, PzKfz IIIs began mounting a short 5cm gun. The Chrysler M2A1 contract was cancelled the same month it was let, and a new contract was granted for 1,000 M3s. The existing M2A1s were used as training tanks.

In June 1940 the M3 tank design was outlined and later standardized on July 11 without a completed design, much less a prototype. In the rush to produce it, the tank was never assigned a developmental "T" designation. European battlefield reports led to the sponson-mounted 75mm being added during its design. Its traverse limitations were understood, but no conventional turret capable of housing it was available.

The Ordnance Department had promised M3 plans to Chrysler by November 1940, but they did not arrive until February 1941. The first hand-built pilot model was run out on April 12 and shipped to Aberdeen Proving Grounds in Maryland on May 3. The tank arsenal commenced production in July 1941 with the first production model completed on July 8. An additional order for 1,200 M3s was placed that month.

In the same month that the M3 contract was let, the design of the T6 (M4) Sherman medium tank was submitted. An M4 prototype was delayed until the M3 entered production. The M4's design was approved in April 1941 with the goal of rapidly mass-producing a fast, reliable tank. The design borrowed heavily from the M3 and incorporated improvements learned from British experience in Africa. Borrowing from the M3's design helped speed up development and made it easier to convert production lines. The first pilot M4 was turned out in September, standardized in October, and full production began in February 1942. It would replace the M3 by August 1943.

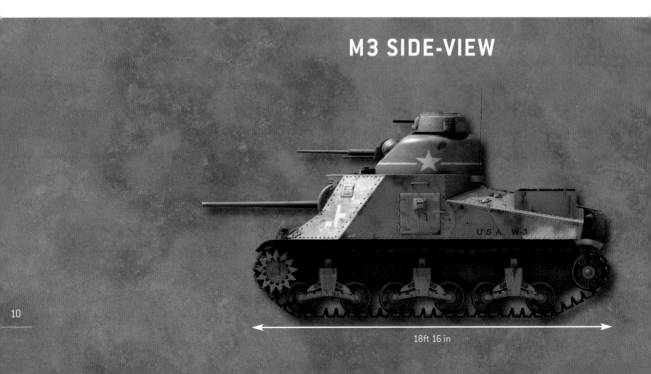

M3 SIDE-VIEW

18ft 16 in

M3 LAYOUT

Most medium tanks of the era, including the PzKpfz III, were laid out similarly. The 360-degree revolving turret was situated just forward of center. It mounted the tank's main gun plus a coaxial machine gun. The turret was manned by the tank commander, gunner, and loader. The driver and radio operator were in the forward portion of the hull; the latter was also the bow machine gunner. The engine was in the rear, protected by a heavy, ventilating louvered cover. The fuel tanks were usually on either side of the engine. Most tank designers strove to maintain a low profile and to incorporate as much sloped armor as possible to improve the armor's ballistic efficiency.

The M3 deviated significantly from the typical tank layout. The most noticeable feature of the 31-ton M3 was its inordinately high profile, due to its secondary gun turret and commander's cupola. The mounting of the main gun in a right front sponson and the secondary gun mounted on a small turret also deviated much from conventional tank design. While the glacis was well sloped, much of the superstructure was only slightly angled or vertical, especially the sides and rear of the superstructure and hull.

The driver sat on the centerline, rather higher than most drivers. This gave him a better field of observation but with greater exposure. To his left were two fixed bow machine guns. After June 1942 the leftmost gun was deleted as being redundant. One or two M2 tripods were provided for dismounted use. A large driver's hatch with an indirect vision device was set at head level. Early M3s had only a vision slit that could be used as an awkward exit hatch. Beside the driver's left shoulder was an observation/pistol port. In the right front portion of the hull was the main gun, either an M2 or M3 75mm gun on an M1 mount. This was a large, horizontally rotating curved shield for traversing, and set in it was the smaller, elevating gun shield. The

The 2d Battalion, 13th Armored Regiment was the only US unit in the Kasserine Pass battles equipped with M3 mediums bearing lustreless olive drab paint (OD No. 9: 33070), often partly camouflaged by hand-smeared mud. The unit still used the January 1942 Armored Force specified identification of yellow stars and a band on the turret as less conspicuous markings; most units had reverted to white. The vertical bar identified the battalion with a short horizontal bar on the right: top Co D, middle Co E, and lower Co F. The detached bar to the left identified the platoon, 3d Platoon if at the bottom. The white tank number is painted on the glacis.

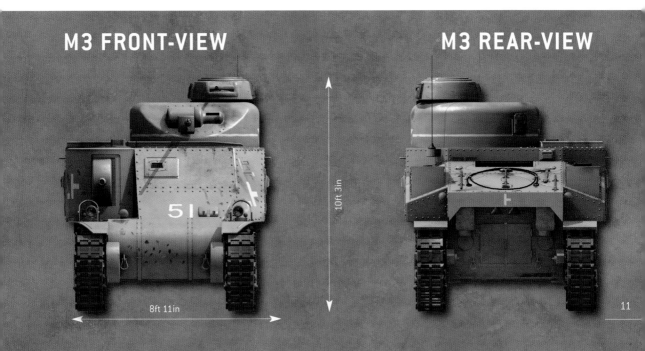

M3 FRONT-VIEW　　　　**M3 REAR-VIEW**

51

10ft 3in

8ft 11in

This photograph clearly illustrates the M3 Grant tank on the left with the larger British-designed turret, and the M3 Lee on the right with the American-designed turret. (Patton Museum)

gunner sat to the gun's left and the assistant gunner behind him. The gunner aimed using an M1 periscope with an integral M21 telescope situated in the top of the hull, but an M15 optical sight was later mounted beside the gun. A hatch was positioned over the assistant gunner's seat. The radio operator sat behind the driver, just forward of the turret. This became the assistant gunner's seat after the radio operator was deleted, at which time the driver took over as radio operator. This conserved manpower, but increased the driver's workload. On both sides of the superstructure were escape hatches with inset observation/pistol ports. These ports were fitted with bulletproof glass vision blocks called "protectoscopes." An observation/pistol port was set in the right rear of the superstructure over the engine compartment. M3A3s and later models had the side escape hatches welded shut, and an escape hatch was provided in the belly, but this made it more vulnerable to mines. These side hatches allowed spalling – bullet and shell fragments – to enter through seams. The secondary gun turret was on a 54.5in.-diameter ring with a well-sloped front and offset to the left rear of the superstructure. The 37mm M5 or M6 gun on an M24 combination mount had a machine gun fitted to the right and the sight to the left. The commander was to the left of the 37mm and had a cupola atop the turret, mounting a machine gun in the right side and a vision port in the left. The cupola could be rotated independently of the turret. Being manual it was too slow to effectively track aircraft, its intended purpose. The commander's seat was fitted

Only 300 of the cast hull M3A1 were built. Later variants of M4 Sherman tanks would use the cast hull.

inside the turret, but the 37mm gunner's seat was on the turret floor to the gun's left and the assistant gunner's to the right of the gun on the turret shield. An observation/pistol port was set in the turret's right rear quadrant. The turret crew was separated from the fighting compartment by a circular shield extending down into the super-structure. There were ventilators aft of the assistant gunner's hatch atop the superstructure, to the left of the driver on the roof, and on the right top of the turret. Flat equipment boxes were fitted to the glacis below the driver's port and over his roof and two large boxes on the sides of the engine deck. There were often removed.

M3 ENGINE AND AMMUNITION

The five-speed transmission was in the forward portion of the hull, with the propeller shaft running beneath the floor back to the engine. The auxiliary power generator, providing electrical power to operate the turret, radio, and lights when the engine was shut down, was in the back of the fighting compartment. The engine was in the rear hull with the air-cooled radiator aft and fuel tanks containing 175gal on either side The engine was accessed through rear twin doors on most models.

A substantial amount of ammunition was carried in the M3: 46 rounds of 75mm, 178 rounds of 37mm, 9,200 rounds of .30cal for the three or four machine guns, 1,200 rounds of .45cal for the two Thompson submachine guns and six pistols, and 12 hand grenades (4xMk II fragmentation, 4xMk III offensive, 2xAN/M8 white smoke for screening, and 2xM14 thermite for destroying the guns if abandoned).

The Chrysler production line at the Detroit Tank Arsenal. Here the final M3A5s are being completed and M4 Sherman production would soon begin.

M3 VARIANTS

M3 production began in August 1941, and there were six US variants of the M3 tank. Five companies produced the variants, which were mostly of riveted construction. The bow was cast in three sections and riveted together, common to all variants. The 37mm turret and cupola were cast on all models. The M3 was powered by a Continental R-975-EC2 or EC1 radial aircraft engine. This was a nine-cylinder engine, burning 92-octane gasoline. The same engine powered the M3A1 and M3A2 variants. The M3 saw the largest production run and was the only one to see combat in US hands in Africa. It could be fitted with either 75mm M2 or M3 guns and 37mm M5 or M6 guns. M3 production ceased in August 1942.

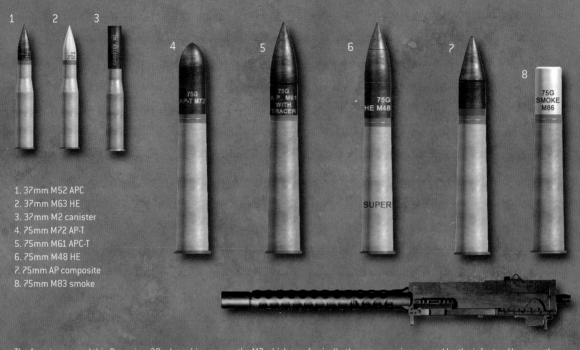

1. 37mm M52 APC
2. 37mm M63 HE
3. 37mm M2 canister
4. 75mm M72 AP-T
5. 75mm M61 APC-T
6. 75mm M48 HE
7. 75mm AP composite
8. 75mm M83 smoke

The Americans used this Browning .30cal machine gun on the M3 which was basically the same version as used by the infantry. However, the tank version was designated "fixed," fitted as a coaxial gun or inside the commander's cupola. Ammunition was issued in cans containing 250 rounds in web belts with one trace (red tip) per four ball or AP (black tip) rounds.

This crew seems to be making jest of the older and smaller 75mm M72 AP-T round held by the second man from the left. Most hold the new M61 APC-T rounds while the middle man holds an M48 HE round. Note the muzzle counterweight on the M5 gun.

The M3A1 was the only model with an entirely cast hull and was otherwise identical to the M3. Only a comparatively small number were produced between February and August 1942. While most had the same engine as the M3, 28 had Guiberson T-1400-2 diesel engines and were designated the M3A1 (Diesel). Only 12 M3A2s were built between January and March 1942, all with welded hulls and otherwise identical to the M3A1. The M3A2 was essentially a prototype for the M3A3.

Only just over 900 M3A3s and M3A5s were produced between January and December 1942, differing only in the M3A3 having a welded hull and the M3A5 a riveted one. Both had General Motors 6046 diesel engines in order to free up aircraft engines. The GM 6046 comprised two GM 6-71 truck engines linked together. Another difference from the diesel-engined models was that engine access was via a lower plate and a pair of louvered top deck doors. The variant that deviated the most was the riveted-hull M3A4, with just over one hundred built between June and August

NICKNAMING AMERICAN TANKS

When the British began purchasing American-made tanks in 1940, they bestowed upon them nicknames based on the names of American Civil War generals as an easy means of identification. While designated, for example, General Grant, they were commonly called the "Grant." These names were adopted informally by the Americans but never officially. Tankers simply called them "M3" or "M4." The terms "Lee" and "Sherman" were seldom used by American tankers. US tanks commonly used by the Commonwealth in North Africa included:

M3-series Stuart light tanks
M3-series Lee medium tanks
M3-series Grant medium tanks (Lee with UK-modified turret)
M4-series Sherman medium tanks
M5-series Stuart light tanks (aka "Honey")

American numeric model designations can be confusing. Since the 1930s the United States designated light and medium tank series beginning with M1. This resulted in both light and medium tanks being used in North Africa that were designated the M3 (another reason the British bestowed nicknames). To break the chain of confusion, M4 was skipped for the next light tank, resulting in the M5, to prevent confusion with the M4 medium tank. (There is no hyphen in US weapon/equipment designations.)

1942. In another effort to eliminate the need for aircraft engines, it was provided with a Chrysler A-57 gasoline engine. This was actually five automobile engines mounted in a star pattern and meshed together, totaling 30 cylinders. This required the rear hull to be extended 14in. resulting in 6in. wider gaps between the suspension bogies.

M3 medium tank production, August 1941–December 1942

Company	M3	M3A1	M3A2	M3A3	M3A4	M3A5
American Locomotive Co.	385	300	-	-	-	-
Baldwin Locomotive Works	295	-	12	322	-	591
Chrysler Detroit Tank Arsenal	3,243	-	-	-	109	-
Pressed Steel Car Co.	501	-	-	-	-	-
Pullman Standard Manufacturing Co.	500	-	-	-	-	-
Total	4,924	300	12	322	109	591

One of the 10 PzKpfw III Ausf A light tanks built for testing in May 1937. None of these saw combat service.

THE PZKPFW III

In 1935 the new German Panzer-Divisionen were being equipped with machine gun-armed PzKpfw I and II light tanks. Originally envisioned only as training tanks while more potent light and medium tanks were developed, they were, in fact, the most common tanks employed in Poland, the Low Countries, and France, along with impounded Czechoslovak tanks. The Panzer I and II also saw use in Africa. In January 1934 the Heereswaffenamt (Army Weapons Office) held a conference attended by representatives of the Kraftfahrkamptruppen (Motorized Battle Troops) to determine the requirements for future light and infantry support (medium) *Panzerkampfwagen* (armor battle vehicles) – tanks. These new tanks had an upper weight limit of 24 metric tons (26.5 US tons) owing to European bridge limitations. Knowing enemy tank armor was certain to improve, German tankers desired a 5cm gun on the light tank. The Army Weapons Office and artillery wanted the 3.7cm gun for ammunition compatibility, the same as the new infantry antitank gun, and not have to allocate production lines to another weapon. To conserve resources this was agreed to, but the design had to incorporate a turret and a 150cm (59in.) turret ring capable of mounting a 5cm in the future. The medium tank would mount a short-barreled 7.5cm.

The development of the new tanks was done secretly to mask German rearmament. It would be conducted under cover designations as the *leichttraktor* and *mittlerestraktor* (light and medium tractors) with the project designation *Vollkettenfraftfahrzeug*

(experimental tracked motorized vehicle) *2000*. The tanks were also bestowed the cover designations of *Zugführerwagen* and *Bataillonsführerwagen* (platoon and battalion commander vehicles). These tanks would become the PzKpfw III light and IV medium, to be popularly known to the Allies as the Mk III and Mk IV tanks, designations given by the British. The German tanker simply called them the Panzer III and Panzer IV, or *Panzer drei* and *Panzer vier*.

Daimler-Benz A.G., Henschel, Krupp, Maschinenfabrik Augsburg-Nürnburg (MAN), and Rheinmetall-Borsig were requested to submit proposals in 1935. The design submitted by Daimler-Benz at Berlin/Marienfelde was selected. Prototypes included the better aspects of the Henschel and MAN designs and were tested between 1936 and 1937 at the Ulm, Sennelager, Döllersheim, and Kummersdorf automotive proving grounds while gun testing took place at Meppen.

The PzKpfw III was of conventional design similar to the Krupp PzKpfw IV, which was actually fielded before the PzKpfw III. From a distance it was difficult to tell the two apart (PzKpfw III had six bogie wheels and the PzKpfw IV had eight). Efforts were also made to make some components interchangeable between the two. The PzKpfw III was assigned the *Sonderkraftfahrzeug* (special motorized vehicle) designation of SdKfz 141.[3]

Another view of a PzKpfw III Ausf A. The six bogie wheels of later models were smaller than this prototype's.

---

3   The SdKfz category designation was assigned to most standard German military vehicles, 101–200 being assigned to full-tracked combat vehicles.

PZKPFW III LAYOUT

The bow of the PzKpfw III was blunt and boxy with a vertically stepped front compartment. The driver was on the left and the radio operator on the right with a ball-mounted machine gun. On the forward horizontal deck over their knees were small break servicing hatches that could be used as escape hatches. The driver had a shuttered vision port with "armored" binoculars, and small vision/pistol ports were on both sides of the forward portion of the superstructure. A small escape hatch was set in the lower hull sides above the bogie wheels and between the first and second return rollers. These were deleted with the Ausf M.[4] The three-man turret had a heavy gun mantlet mounting the main gun with two coaxial machine guns to the right in the Ausf A to C and the sight to the left. Later versions had one coaxial gun. The turret sides were gently sloped and the back slightly rounded. There were vent/pistol ports on the forward sides and split door escape hatches on both sides of the turret's rear sides, each with a vision port. The vision ports/slits were protected by bulletproof glass blocks. In the rear center of the turret top was the raised commander's "dustbin-type" cupola with a split hatch on top. Five vision slits provided 360-degree observation. The gunner sat to the gun's left, and the loader, who also operated the coaxial machine gun by a foot-peddle trigger, sat to the right. The gunner manually rotated the turret, and the loader had an auxiliary traverse handle. The commander and gunner had seats mounted on the turret wall, but the loader did not. There was no turret floor, so the loader had to walk on the hull floor as the turret traversed.

---

4   Ausf stands for *Ausführung* (version), a letter appended to the PzKpfw designation identifying a sub-variant.

Panzer-Regiment 7 tanks were painted yellow-brown (RAL 8000), sometimes with the original dark gray (RAL 7027) showing through. Sometimes about 20 percent of the tank was splotched with gray-green (RAL 7008). Sometimes continental-painted tanks were merely coated with used oil and dusted with sand. The company number was painted in black on the turret side, Kompanie 4, with the tank number in smaller characters. The regimental insignia is seen on the equipment bin behind the turret. The Balkenkreuz (beamed cross) is on the hull and was often partly obscured by mud or lightly sprayed paint.

PZKPFW III SIDE-VIEW

18ft 2in.

PZKPFW III AMMUNITION

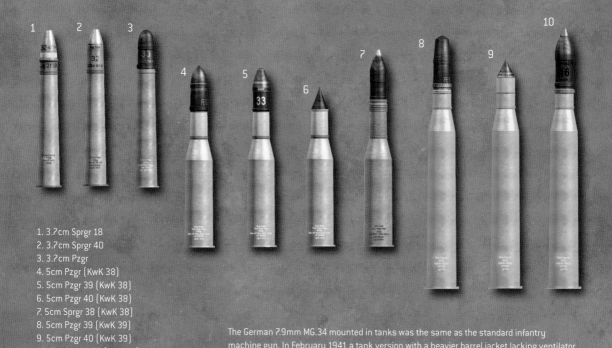

1. 3.7cm Sprgr 18
2. 3.7cm Sprgr 40
3. 3.7cm Pzgr
4. 5cm Pzgr (KwK 38)
5. 5cm Pzgr 39 (KwK 38)
6. 5cm Pzgr 40 (KwK 38)
7. 5cm Sprgr 38 (KwK 38)
8. 5cm Pzgr 39 (KwK 39)
9. 5cm Pzgr 40 (KwK 39)
10. 5cm Sprgr 38 (KwK 39) 7

The German 7.9mm MG.34 mounted in tanks was the same as the standard infantry machine gun. In February 1941 a tank version with a heavier barrel jacket lacking ventilator holes was authorized for installation in new production tanks. Standard combat ammunition was the "bullet with steel core" (black tip, red rimmed primer) as opposed to lead cores to achieve better penetration. The recoil-operated gun fired at 800–900 rpm.

PZKPFW III FRONT-VIEW

PZKPFW III REAR-VIEW

8ft 2in.

9ft 8in.

The engine was in the rear, accessible through upper deck hatches, along with changing arrangements of air ventilators. This engine was a Maybach HL108TR 12-cylinder, 300-horsepower gasoline. The transmission was ten-speed, although later a six-speed was introduced to ease the driver's workload. The two fuel tanks were on either side of the engine in the Ausf A to C, carrying 125 liters (33gal), while later models had four tanks that held 320 liters (85gal). The air-cooled radiators, exhaust, and muffler systems were in the hull's rear.

Numerous modifications were introduced during the PzKpfw III's production including changes to the cupola, gun mantlet, hatches, vision/pistol ports, escape hatches, armor skirts, air intakes, engine covers and hatches, spaced armor arrangements, and headlights, among others. Changes were also made to the six bogie wheels, three return rollers, rear idle wheels, and front drive sprockets in efforts to correct roughriding suspension problems that effected gun accuracy. Track width was 36cm (14.1in.) with 99 links, later widened to 40cm (15.7in.) with the Ausf H.

Ten of the first model, the PzKpfw III Ausf A, were built from May 1937 followed by 15 each Bs and Cs and then 30 Ds, used for troop trials into 1938. From 1938 to 1939, 96 Ausf Es were built. Only 98 PzKpfw IIIs and just over twice that many PzKpfw IVs were available in September 1939. Large-scale production did not begin until 435 Ausf Fs were built from 1939 to 1940 and used in France. Frontal armor upgrades were implemented on the Ausf D and later models. Later versions were built in the hundreds until the introduction of the Ausf J in 1941 with over 2,600 built. The PzKpfw III and components were produced by Daimler-Benz A.G., Henschel und Sonn A.G., Altmaerkische Kettenwerk, GmbH, Waggonfabrik Wegmann A.G., Muehlenbau und Industrie A.G., Maschinenfabrik Augsburg Nuernburg A.G., and Maschinenfabrik Niedersachen Hannover GmbH.

The PzKpfw III Ausf A to E, and some Ausf Fs were armed with a 3.7cm Kwk 36 L/45 gun. As foreseen, a larger caliber weapon was needed, and so the short-barreled 5cm KwK 38 L/42 was used on the Ausf F to H from June 1940. The 3.7cm was found inadequate against heavily armored French tanks such as the Char B, leading to it being called the *Türklopfer* (doorknocker). Existing PzKpfw IIIs were to be upgraded by December, but this was not completed as there were still outstanding requests for upgrading in June 1941. From early 1942 later Ausf Js were armed with the long 5cm KwK 39 L/60 gun as were the Ausf L and M, after experiencing the Soviet T-34 in summer 1941. The Germans differentiated between the two 5cm gun models by calling them a PzKpfw III *kurz* (short) and *lang* (long). The Ausf N of July 1942, the last version, had the 7.5cm KwK 37 L/24 short gun as originally mounted on the PzKpfw IV. Its primary role was to protect Tiger tanks.

By 1942 the roles of the PzKpfw III and IV were reversed. The lighter PzKpfw III became the infantry support tank, and the PzKpfw IV

PzKpfw III light tank production, 1937–43		
Ausführung	Number	Years
A	10	1937
B	15	1937
C	15	1937–38
D	30	1938
E	96	1938–39
F	435	1939–40
G	600	1940–41
H	308	1940–41
J (5cm L/42)	1,549	1941–42
J (5cm L/60)	1,067	1942
L	653	1942
M	250	1942–43
N	660	1942–43
Total	5,688	

Ausf H with a long high-velocity 7.5cm KwK 40 L/48 gun was the main medium tank intended to take on other tanks. The PzKpfw III was the second most produced German tank being surpassed by the PzKpfw IV.

PZKPFW AMMUNITION

The early models were armed with a 3.7cm gun and twin coaxial machine guns with 120 rounds of 3.7cm and 4,435 rounds of 7.9mm for the three machine guns. Those with one coaxial gun had 2,700 rounds, although the Ausf L and M carried 3,750 rounds. A quantity of 9mm ammunition was carried for the crew's five pistols and one submachine gun as were hand grenades and 24 2.6cm flare pistol cartridges. The 5cm gun-armed tanks had 99 rounds (typical load was 58 HE, 36 AP, and 5 AP40 rounds) until the Ausf J with 84, and the Ausf L and M carried 92. The number of storage bins is misleading as to the number of rounds actually carried. A British examination of two abandoned PzKpfw IIIs in Tunisia revealed that besides the 99 bins, one had another 86 rounds stacked on the floor, and the other had 83 to total 185 and 182 rounds, respectively. One tank carried 98 AP and 80 HE while the other had 111 AP and 51 HE. A few from the bins had been fired and other loose rounds may have been before the tanks were captured. In comparison to Allied tanks which carried a high percentage of AP, the Germans carried a high percentage of HE to use against soft-skin vehicles, stone-constructed fighting positions (sangars), and personnel.

THE STRATEGIC SITUATION

The seesaw war in North Africa had been tottering back and forth since September 1940 when Italian forces in Libya attempted a reluctant and cautious advance into Egypt. The numerically inferior defending Commonwealth Western Desert Force quickly stalled the attack. The British launched an offensive in December 1940, driving back the surprised Italians into Libya and shattering much of the Italian force.

The Italian route was not able to be vigorously exploited owing to insufficient reserves, but the British gained a foothold in Libya. Commonwealth forces were reinforced in January 1941, and the offensive resumed. The Italians were routed, and there was no doubt of their inability to wage modern warfare. Axis attacks subsequently commenced on British-held Malta. The Axis failure to take Malta aided in their eventual defeat in the Mediterranean as Allied air and naval operations launched from there greatly hampered Axis resupply and reinforcement efforts. Tobruk soon fell to the British, and by early February the Italians had been driven from Cyrenaica (northeast Libya) and largely destroyed.

Mussolini, totally humiliated by the easy defeat of his forces and the loss of his African territory, asked Hitler for assistance. On February 12 General Rommel arrived in Tripoli as German forces prepared to deploy there. Tripoli in French Algeria had become the main Axis logistics base after the loss of Tobruk when the British moved into Libya. The 5. leichte Division began arriving equipped with PzKpfw I, II, III, and IV tanks. On February 24 German and

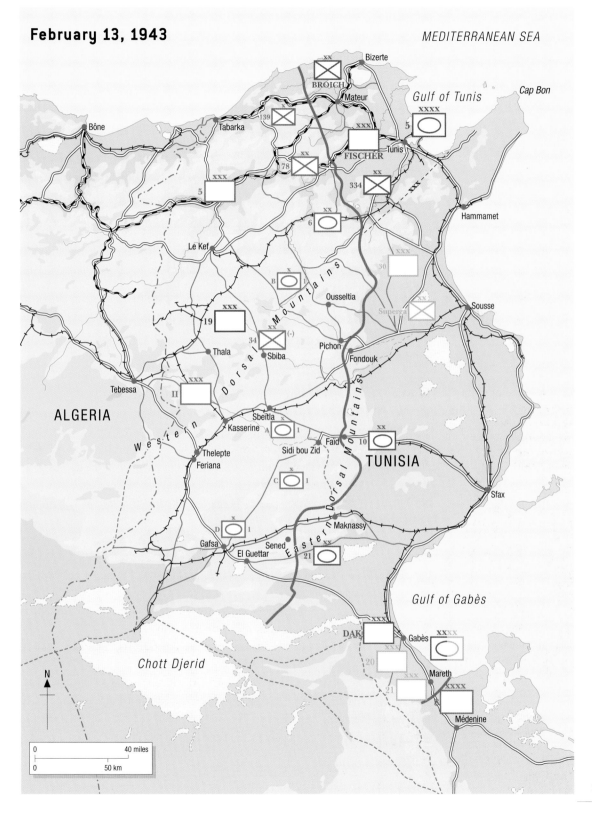

February 13, 1943

MEDITERRANEAN SEA

Cap Bon

Bizerte

BROICH

Mateur

Gulf of Tunis

Bône

Tabarka

139

5

Tunis

FISCHER

78

334

Hammamet

5

6

Le Kef

30

Ousseltia

Superga

Sousse

B

19

Mountains

34 (-)

Pichon

Fondouk

Thala

Sbiba

Western   Dorsal   Mountains

Eastern Dorsal Mountains

Tebessa

II

ALGERIA

Sbeïtla

Kasserine

A

10

Faïd

TUNISIA

Sfax

Thelepte

Feriana

Sidi bou Zid

C

D

Gafsa

Maknassy

Sened

21

El Guettar

Gulf of Gabès

DAK

Gabès

20

21

Mareth

Médenine

Chott Djerid

N

| 0 | | 40 miles |
| 0 | | 50 km |

23

British patrols made their first contact, just six days before the Deutsches Afrikakorps was established. In late March Rommel made his first advance against understrength and poorly equipped Commonwealth forces. Rommel had been directed to hold, but he attacked, even though told he knew full well that he would not receive any supplies. In less than two weeks, the German and Italian forces had pushed back the British and isolated Tobruk. Libya was reclaimed, and German patrols probed into Egypt. The supply situation prevented further advances, and the tottering Commonwealth forces were reinforced. The 15. Panzer-Division began arriving between April and June. The British began to gradually reinforce their forces in mid-May, but at the end of the month, the Germans took Halfaya Pass, establishing a foothold in Egypt. A lull followed as both forces built up supplies. At the beginning of June, the Vichy French allowed the Germans to use Bizerta just inside Algeria to deliver "nonmilitary" supplies. In mid-June the British launched a major offensive to relieve Tobruk, but within a few days they lost the initiative and Rommel retained Halfaya Pass. A long stalemate ensured, and both sides built up forces and supplies in preparation for the next battle. In September the British Eighth Army was activated to control Commonwealth forces in the Western Desert. The 5. leichte Division was redesignated 21. Panzer-Division on October 1, and the 90. leiche Afrika-Division arrived. However, it was not until November that the British offensive was launched, foiling Rommel's planned attack on Tobruk. Both sides battered themselves severely, and the Tobruk breakout attempt failed. Fighting continued into December with Tobruk almost reached. It was at this point that the United States entered the war. After suffering heavy losses Rommel began an orderly withdrawal.

In early January 1942 the Germans received replacement tanks, including many PzKpfw IIIs, and the British began withdrawing forces to redeploy to the Far East. The British advance continued with pockets of Axis troops surrendering. Rommel secretly planned a counteroffensive without informing higher commands, and he reversed direction, counterattacking on January 21, 1942. Within three weeks he had recovered most lost ground and shattered Commonwealth forces, which were in retreat, but dug in at Galzala west of Tobruk. Another lengthy stalemate ensued. Then in late

The only battalion of the 1st Armored Division to be deployed into combat with the older M3 medium tank was the 2/13th Armored with one of its tanks pictured here in December 1942 in the race for Tunis. The rest of the 1st Armored Division had already been re-supplied with M4A1 Shermans by this stage of the war. (NARA)

May Rommel launched a new offensive. The British positions were well fortified, but the German–Italian armor attempted to outflank them. The British armor was deployed for such an eventuality but was too widely dispersed and was outmaneuvered. However, within three days the Axis armor was out of fuel. Rommel was forced to pull back and form a "cauldron" to beat off British attacks. The Germans managed to keep their supply lines open, and the fighting went on into June with the British suffering heavy armor losses. After fighting off superior Commonwealth forces in a defensive battle, the now superior in armor Germans pursued the fleeing remnants. Tobruk fell to the Germans on June 21, giving them huge stocks of fuel and rations. Two days later German troops crossed the Egyptian frontier. It was here in the Galzala Line battle that the Germans first confronted the M3 Grant. The Eighth Army began establishing a defensive line at El Alamein. By July 4 Rommel had finally been halted and had few tanks remaining. Aware of severe German shortages, the British launched local attacks to keep the Germans, and especially the Italians, off balance, forcing them to expend more resources. The fighting went into July when both sides regrouped. The Germans continued to experience great difficulty in receiving supplies owing to attacks from British-held Malta.

In August it was decided to place General Eisenhower in command of the planned northwest Africa invasion, Operation *Torch*, at the same time Montgomery took command of Eighth Army. At the end of August Rommel launched an attack to drive the British from Egypt, but British preparations were well underway, their artillery was more effectively organized, and the RAF dominated the sky. Rommel, still short of supplies, was counting on promised shipments. Within four days the German attack stalled, and they were forced to withdraw to their original positions. Montgomery, still armor poor, wisely decided not to pursue, husbanding his resources for his future offensive. Discovering the British were sending massive reinforcements, Rommel prepared elaborate defenses. However, on September 23 Rommel was forced to fly to Germany for medical treatment, and General Stumme assumed temporary command. To replace the large officer losses suffered by the Afrikakorps, officers were transferred from the Eastern Front, but many did not fit in with the freewheeling desert veterans and the ways of the desert, lacking the chivalrous attitude of the *alte Afrikaner soldaten.*

A NEW FRONT IN NORTHWEST AFRICA

In October 1942 the Operation *Torch* convoys departed the United States and the United Kingdom bound for northwest Africa. Negotiations were undertaken with Vichy French officers and officials in Algeria in an effort to prevent resistance, but they were not successful and British participation was minimal owing to extreme French animosity. On October 23 Montgomery attacked at El Alamein with a 2-1 superiority, creating a great deal of confusion and it was here that the M4 Sherman made its combat debut. General Stumme died of a heart attack, and Rommel was ordered back to Africa but did not arrive until December 3. The British continued the fight, and the Germans were forced to commence withdrawing on November 3. Although Hitler ordered a halt, the Germans, after suffering huge losses, had no choice but to continue their withdrawal. In the western Mediterranean, German and Italian submarines were concentrated owing to the arrival of Allied shipping at Gibraltar. This was assessed as a buildup for a Malta reinforcement attempt. On November 8 the Allies landed at multiple points near Casablanca on the Atlantic coast of Morocco and on the Mediterranean coast of Algeria around Oran and Algiers. Tunisia was over 400 miles to the east of the latter. After token resistance the French signed an armistice on the 11th, and that same day Hitler ordered Vichy France occupied. The day after the landing, German reinforcements began pouring into Tunisia from Sicily to face this new front behind Rommel. The British began their westward advance through Libya and recaptured Tobruk on the 12th. French troops in Tunisia began withdrawing from the coastal towns to join the Allies as British and US troops entered the country on the 15th. On the 18th British units in Tunisia made their first contact with Germans. Allied forces in Tunisia made limited, cautious progress and by the 27th were only 15 miles from Tunis. But the German defenses proved to be strong, and they managed limited counterattacks as they built up their forces flowing in from Europe. Some of these German counterattacks were successful, but others were beaten back. The 10. Panzer-Division began arriving in Tunisia in late November. On December 11 the Eighth Army again began to advance into Libya. The Germans soon retreated to avoid being outflanked. In western Tunisia V British Corps in the north continued its attacks while the II US Corps in the south broke off its own. By late December 1942 rain and poor visibility were hampering both sides' operations.

The first week of February 1943 found the Allies in control of a little over half of northern Tunisia arrayed from north to south. The 139th Infantry Brigade, 78th Infantry Division; the 6th Armoured Division under V British Corps; Combat Command B, 34th Infantry Division (-); and the 1st Armored Division's Command Commands A, C, and D under II US Corps were thinly spread to the north shore of the Chott el Djerid, a dry salt lake. The Germans misidentified the 1st Armored Division as the 2d due to poor intelligence when, in fact, the 2d Armored Division was still in Morocco. The XIX French Corps was in reserve west of the 34th US Infantry Division. The 1st US Infantry Division was broken up among different commands to augment their infantry. The number of Allied units at the front was limited by the transportation available to move supplies forward.

The 5. Panzer-Armee under General der Panzertruppen Hans-Jügen von Arnim, Hitler's new favorite after Rommel's defeat at El Alamein, was deployed in the north with Korpsgruppe Fischer comprised of 10. Panzer-Division, 334. Infanterie-Division, and Division von Broich. The Italian XXX Corpo had only one infantry division and a couple of regimental-sized units. The 21. Panzer-Division was directly under the Panzer-Armee. Rommel commanded the Deutsche-Italienische Panzerarmee in the south with the Afrikakorps now under Generalleutnant Hans Cramer. It contained 15. Panzer-Division, an Italian armored division, and a Luftwaffe infantry brigade. There were also two Italian corps, XX and XXI Corpo, each with two Italian infantry divisions and a German light Africa division to stiffen them. The 90. was with XX Corpo, and the 164. was with XXI Corpo. Most of this army was defending the old French defensive line at Mareth, holding off Eighth Army. However, 10. and 21. Panzer-Divisionen were positioning themselves to test the Americans who were defending Faïd Pass. Both divisions relied on the PzKpfw III.

Damaged and abandoned Panzer IIIs. Possession of the field at the end of battle was critical giving the victor the chance not only to recover and repair equipment but also the opportunity to examine the enemy's tanks and vehicles.

THE TACTICAL SITUATION

The battle for Kasserine Pass was actually a series of engagements that lasted from the end of January through February 1943, cumlinating in the battle of El Guettar on March 23, 1943, the first significant US victory over German armor.

The Germans and Italians in northeast Tunisia were holding back the British who were less than 40 miles from Tunis, the vital Axis supply port and potential evacuation point. The Axis had little operational depth. Their western defensive line ran along the low Eastern Dorsal Mountains, roughly paralleling Tunisia's east coast. The Germans would have preferred to add depth to the defense by holding the higher Western Dorsal Mountains somewhat further inland, but lacked the necessary forces. Far to the south Italian infantry and the Afrikakorps were dug in on the narrow frontage of the Mareth Line. There the Eighth Army was unable to resume the offensive because of its overstretched supply lines. Only 60 miles to the northwest were thinly stretched elements of the 1st US Armored Division on an 80-mile front. It was relying on its mobility and the generally moderate terrain to respond to attacks.

At the end of January 1943 a series of skirmishes, raids, and spoiling attacks were undertaken by both sides around Faïd and points south. Both were attempting to keep their opponents off balance as they built up their forces and tried to seize terrain to give them a tactical advantage and from which to launch future advances. The first move was for the Germans to launch a spoiling attack at Faïd Pass, which was weakly held by the French. Just prior to the attack the Americans to the southwest executed a raid on Sened Station, driving off the Italian defenders. On January 30 two 21. Panzer-Division battle groups attacked Faïd Pass and Rebaou Pass, 4 miles to the south. The American response was confused with senior American commanders too far to the rear to appraise the situation and lacking sufficient forces to support the

A view of the rugged terrain around Kasserine Pass. This perspective shows the view from the west looking towards the narrowest part of the pass. However, during the 1943 battle this dry riverbed would have been in full flood. (Patton Museum)

French who were now caught between two *Kampfgruppen* (battle groups). The Americans only sent patrols to report on the situations at Faïd and Rebaou. Finding them occupied, Task Forces Stark and Kern were dispatched from the west to attack Faïd and Rebaou. Combat Command C (CCC) to the southwest was directed to head northeast to Sidi Bou Zid to the west of the two passes as a backup. The two task forces were too small to deal with the prepared German defenses and suffered losses from dug-in 8.8cm guns, and the January 30 and February 1 attacks were repulsed. In the meantime, CCC, on its way to Sidi Bou Zid, was ordered to turn south and attack Maknassy. Yet it too was repulsed by Germans dug in north of its objective. The Germans had by now determined that the Americans were thinly spread, suffered from poor control, and were still inexperienced. Axis commanders saw the situation as an opportunity to execute larger-scale attacks and to further exploit the green American and French troops, keep them off balance to gain time, and deal with the more pressing threat of the British to the north. This led to a flurry of competing Axis plans.

Generaloberst Jürgen von Armin, commanding 5. Panzer-Armee, proposed Operation *Kuckuchsei* (Cuckoo's Egg), an attack against the British right flank in an effort to separate them from the Americans and French. Rommel thought this plan was too limiting. Understanding the Allied weaknesses and the Mareth Line being stable for the moment, he wished to use the Eastern Dorsals position to attack toward the western mountains and Kasserine Pass. Once seizing the pass, he could continue to the American forward supply base at Tébessa or threaten the British right flank, a goal he was keen on achieving, believing it would slow their advance. To conduct such an operation, Rommel would need additional mobile forces from 5. Panzer-Armee. General von Armin argued against what he thought was Rommel's overly ambitious plan. The Italian chief of staff, General Ambrosio, reviewed the plans and was inclined toward Rommel's, realizing that Mussolini's image needed a boost after the loss of Libya. However, he did not believe sufficient mobile forces were available to accomplish Rommel's plan. Ambrosio proposed a more limited alternative. Rather than Rommel controlling both armies' mobile forces for a deep attack, he proposed two separate but coordinated attacks. General von Armin would exploit his seizure of Faïd Pass and take Sidi Bou Zid to destroy Combat Command A (CCA) and then seize Kasserine. This would be Operation *Frühlingswind* (Spring Wind). Rommel would make a more limited attack aimed at Gafsa 60 miles southwest of Faïd and defended by Combat Command D (CCD). He would then continue northwest to link up with Armin's force near Thelepte south of Kasserine. This was Operation *Morgenluft* (Morning Breeze). The launch date was left up to von Arnim who was keeping an eye on the rainy weather, which would hamper his air support.

Terrain had much to do with the conduct of the battle. The area around Sidi Bou Zid was mostly flat with few restrictions to cross-country movement. It was a different matter on the terrain immediately around Djebel el Kebar and Djebel Lessouda to the southwest and the north, respectively, of Sidi Bou Zid and Djebel Ksaira to the east. These were low hills, and the gently sloping ground around their bases was cut by countless radiating gullies and rocks. Other low hills lay to the northeast and northwest. The ground was rocky, gravelly, and almost impossible to dig in. Large wadis were few and troops were forced to construct rock sangars for fighting positions. The few roads in the area (Sidi Bou Zid was a crossroads) were single- or "one-and-a-half" lane hard-packed earth. Vegetation was low patches of thorny camel brush, clump grass, and occasional cactus, offering little concealment. The weather was mild in the low 70°F (20°C) range in the day, dropping into the 50°F (10–15°C) range at night. Humidity was about 10–40 percent and it rained sporadically, and although the ground immediately soaked it up, there were some marsh and mud areas.

Tunisia's hills caused problems for the German Western Desert veterans as they tended to underscore their importance. The Americans positioned artillery observers in the hills, and the Germans failed to secure the hills with infantry, of which they were severely short.

The Americans emplaced defensive positions on the plains between the Dorsals and prepared for the spring offensive. By now the Allies had become reliant on Enigma intelligence, especially since it had proved so accurate during El Alamein. However, the intercepted German traffic came from different commands and was sometimes incomplete. Its meaning was often misinterpreted, and therefore imprecise directives were issued to defending units. Most assessments believed the main German attacks would be aimed at the British First Army's southern flank, and the scattered Americans might experience only divisionary attacks. Eisenhower found that various headquarters were too far to the rear, and forward units had not deployed to more favorable positions. To make matters worse, in the immediate Sidi Bou Zid area the infantry were dug in on Djebel Lessouda to the north of the crossroads and on Djebel Ksaira and Garet Hadid to the southeast. These two positions were 7 miles from each other, too far apart for mutual support.

To execute Operation *Frühlingswind,* 10. Panzer-Division moved by a series of night marches from Fairouan to assemble east of Faïd Pass. They were to clear the pass before sunrise. The division's nonmotorized units would take part in the assault on Sidi Bou Zid. Kampfgruppe Gerhardt would be the first through the pass and would swing northwest around Djebel Lessouda to neutralize it and then block any American advances. Kampfgruppe Reimann would advance along the Faïd–Sbeïtla road and swing southwest in two elements to seize Sidi Bou Zid. The division reserve was Kampfgruppe Lang, a motorcycle rifle battalion. Both Panzer divisions' artillery would be massed in the hills east of Faïd. The 21. Panzer-Division to the south would conduct a two-pronged attack with both emerging from Maïzila Pass. Kampfgruppe Schuette would attack north on the Maïzila–Sidi Bou Zid road as a supporting attack and drive defenders into the village. The stronger Kampfgruppe Stenkhoff would emerge from the pass and strike 25 miles cross-country toward Bir el Hafey. From there it would turn northeast toward Sidi Bou Zid. These two battle groups would be reinforced by nonmotorized units coming out of Aïn Rebaou Pass just south of Faïd to encircle the remaining Americans.

TECHNICAL
SPECIFICATIONS

M3 MEDIUM TANK

The basic M3 medium tank with a riveted hull was by far the most common model with almost 5,000 built while only 1,334 of the later five variants were produced. The later models were not necessarily qualitative improvements, but rather manufacturing alternatives to speed production or better utilize the capabilities of the manufacturing plants. The M3A1 had a cast hull, and the M3A2 and M3A3 were welded. However, the M3A4 and M3A5 reverted to riveted construction. The M3A3 through M3A5 increased the original 60,000lb weight by a further 3,000–4,000lb. The M3A3 and M3A5 were powered by diesel engines, which did increase the operating range by 40 miles and notched up the speed from 26 to 29mph. There were no or only minor upgrades to increase armor, improve suspension, change armament, increase ammunition storage, improve crew accommodation, or employ more effective observation or sighting gear, nor were there improvements in obstacle- crossing capabilities. What this all amounted to was that the M3A5 was no better than the original M3.

The only notable improvements were in the armament. The 75mm M3 gun, with its longer barrel, was an improvement over the 75mm M2, providing higher velocity and longer range. The 37mm M5 lacked the 37mm M6's automatically opening breech, a valuable feature that the M6 possessed in addition to its 6in. longer barrel. Both the 75mm and 37mm guns were gyrostabilized, which was installed on all tanks from January 1942. The other armament improvement was the removal of one of the

A battalion of M3 medium tanks training at Perham Downs on December 6, 1943.

two fixed bow machine guns. The 2d Battalion, 13th Armored Regiment with M3 tanks carried both M2 and M3 guns. They also possessed early and late variants of the suspension bogies.

The Grant's main gun, mounted in a right side sponson, was the 75mm M2 or M3. The M3 was standardized on July 24, 1941. The M2 was identical to the M3, but its barrel length of 91.7in. was 26.6in. shorter than the 118.4in. M3 barrel. The M2 had a vertically dropping breechlock, and the gun was developed only as an infantry support gun with little concern for high velocity. The M3's longer barrel significantly increased its range and velocity, making it a better tank killer. The M3 gun was developed to artillery standards with a 24,000-round barrel life, it not yet being considered that tanks seldom outlived the barrel. The M2 gun could be found on even the latest model tanks. The 910lb gun had an automatically opening drop-type breechblock. The gun's recoil automatically opened the breechblock, ejected the spent case, locked the breech in the open position, and recocked. The breechblock closed automatically when a round was loaded. The gun could be fired by a solenoid or manual trigger. Its rate of fire was up to 20rpm, but accurate aimed fire was typically 10–12 max. The recoil was about 14in. There were two short recoil cylinders beneath the barrel, and the gunner was protected by a cage-type shoulder guard. The M2 gun mount allowed a +20 degrees elevation, -9 degrees depression, and 15 degrees traverse left and right, all manually. Some, but not all early tanks, were fitted with gyrostabilizers on both guns. The M2 required a ringlike muzzle counterbalance while the longer-barreled M3 did not.

The 37mm M6 gun had been standardized on November 14, 1940, and would be used in the M3-series medium tanks; M3A1, M3A3, M5, and M5A1 light tanks; and the M8 and T17 armored cars. The M6 was an improvement of the M5 gun, itself developed from the infantry's M3A1 towed antitank gun. The M5 was used in earlier M3 mediums. The M6 was fitted with an automatic opening breechblock. It also had a 6in. longer barrel than the M5, slightly increasing its velocity and range. For the M3 medium the M6 was fitted on the M24 combination mount with brackets for a coaxial .30-cal machine gun to the right. Fitted in a cramped turret, it recoiled only 6–8in. It used a drop-type breechblock, and a short recoil cylinder was beneath the 78in. barrel. The gun weighed only 190lb, but with the mount and recoil mechanism it weighed in at 700lb. The M6 could crank out 15–20 aimed shots a minute. The gun elevated to +60 degrees (an unusually high elevation for this type of turret) and depressed -7 degrees. This was accomplished by a handwheel, but a throwout lever allowed the gun to be freely elevated. Turret traverse was hydraulically powered with a backup manual traverse. The 37mm counterbalance was a rodlike projection beneath the barrel.

The suspension system was composed of three bogie assemblies per side with two small road wheels and a return roller at the top. Late production M3s had the roller fitted to a rearward extension and heavier volute springs. Track width was 16 ⁹⁄₁₆in. with 158 T41 links (166 on the M3A4).

The M3 tank was rife with flaws, some fatal. The most predominate drawback was its high profile, a total of 10ft 3in., a moving mountain compared to the M4 Sherman at 9ft or the PzKpfz III and IV, which were only 8.2ft high. While providing excellent observation for the commander and 37mm gunner as well as a superior perch for the 37mm and machine guns, the high profile made the M3 easier to detect and provided a larger target to the enemy. The commander's elevated position also presented a much different perspective from that seen by the driver and 75mm gunner. This difference in view had to be understood by the crew. The commander's job was further made more complex because he had to control two large-caliber guns.

The high profile made it difficult to position the tank in a hull defilade position with just the 37mm turret or the commander's cupola exposed. The main problem was that for the lower-mounted 75mm gun to be allowed to fire over any cover, over half the tank's superstructure was exposed.

Another major problem existed in that the main gun could only fire forward and that the tank had to be oriented toward the target. In an advance, if a target to the flank was to be engaged, the vehicle had to make a turn and halt its forward movement; the gun only had a total traverse of 30 degrees. This also disrupted the platoon's movement formation. During a withdrawal the main gun could only be used if the tank halted and turned or was backing, which greatly slowed the tank down and made it

An M3 shown moving towards the the western end of Kasserine Pass during the early stages of fighting. (NARA)

difficult to prevent the tank from backing into any manmade or natural obstacles and hazards. During Operation *Torch* landing craft that could carry and land the M3 medium were unavail-able. The landing force had to rely on M3 lights, and the mediums had to be off-loaded from transports by boom crane once ports were secured.

While the 2in.-thick glacis armor was well sloped, the degree of slope gave it the equivalent to 4⅜in. The 1.5in. vertical side and rear armor was extremely vulnerable. In some ways its armor was superior to some British tanks, and the frontal armor defeated many of the smaller German antitank weapons. The riveted rolled homogeneous armor also caused problems. An AP projectile striking a rivet head could break it off and cause the rivet shaft to ricochet about the interior with deadly effect.

A problem never solved was the ease at which hits in the engine compartment set the tank alight. The 37mm ammunition was stowed in open racks that lined the turret and turret shield while 75mm rounds were stowed all about the fighting compartment. There were few protective compartments or tubes, making it easy for the ammunition to ignite when struck by hot AP shot fragments. The Russians nicknamed the M3 "communal grave for seven" or "device for incinerating seven brothers." It is worth noting that the M4 Sherman, which the Germans called the *Tommykocher* (Tommy cooker), suffered the same flaw.

Regardless of flaws, the M3 was considered reasonably reliable, was solidly constructed, and had adequate armor. Its greatest value lay in the 75mm gun. Even with its low velocity and traversing problems, it was among the heaviest guns mounted on Allied tanks in North Africa. It came at a time when the Germans were fielding

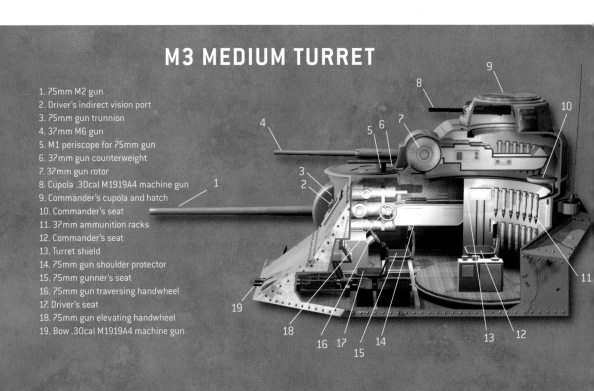

M3 MEDIUM TURRET

1. 75mm M2 gun
2. Driver's indirect vision port
3. 75mm gun trunnion
4. 37mm M6 gun
5. M1 periscope for 75mm gun
6. 37mm gun counterweight
7. 37mm gun rotor
8. Cupola .30cal M1919A4 machine gun
9. Commander's cupola and hatch
10. Commander's seat
11. 37mm ammunition racks
12. Commander's seat
13. Turret shield
14. 75mm gun shoulder protector
15. 75mm gunner's seat
16. 75mm gun traversing handwheel
17. Driver's seat
18. 75mm gun elevating handwheel
19. Bow .30cal M1919A4 machine gun

increasing numbers of PzKpfw IIIs with long 5cm guns and PzKpfw IVs with long 7.5cm guns. German armor did not hold up to the M3's 75mm, credited with knocking out tanks at up to 2,500yd. The 37mm was ineffective against PzKpfw IIIs beyond 500yd unless a bogie or return roller was knocked off.

The June 27, 1943, issue of *Das Reich* ran an article discussing the merits and faults of Allied tanks. It was none too complimentary of the M3:

On Soviet territory English tanks were a failure;[5] and shared this fate with North American tanks, which were not appreciated very much by the Soviet ally. These North American tanks include the "General Stuart" [M3/M5 light], a reconnaissance and rearguard tank, bristling with machine guns, as well as the "General Lee" [M3 medium]. Although the latter possesses commendable motor qualities, its contours are not well balanced, and its silhouette is bizarre and too tall.

---

5   This is reference to their assessment that British tanks, of which almost 5,000 were supplied to the USSR, were better suited for the desert being "adapted to the hot and sparsely settled areas of the English colonial empire" and that a "tank for Europe, apparently, is something the English do not show much talent for."

SPECIFICATIONS: M3 LEE MEDIUM TANK

General
Production run: May 1941–August 1942
Vehicles produced: 4,924
Combat weight: 60,000lb
Crew: Six (commander, 75mm gunner, 37mm gunner, 2x assistant gunners, driver)

Dimensions
Hull length: 18ft 6in.
Width: 8ft 11in.
Height: 10ft 3in.
Ground contact length: 147in.

Armor
Hull front: 2in. (upper), 1.5in. (lower)
Hull sides: 1.5in.
Hull rear: 1.5in.
Hull roof: .5in.
Hull bottom: .5–1in.
Turret front: 2.25in.
Turret sides and rear: 2.25in.
Turret roof: .6in.

Armament
Main gun: 75mm M2 or M3
Secondary gun: 37mm M5 or M6
Machine guns: 3x .30cal M1919A4
Main gun rate of fire: 10–12rpm
Secondary gun rate of fire: 15–20rpm

Ammunition storage
Main gun: 46 rounds
Secondary gun: 178 rounds
Machine guns: 9,200 rounds

Communications
SCR-538 receiver or SCR-528 receiver/transmitter

Motive power
Engine: Continental R-975-EC2 or C1
Power: 240hp at 2,400rpm
Fuel capacity: 175gal

Performance
Maximum road speed: 26mph
Operational range: 120mi
Maximum grade ability: 60 percent
Trench crossing ability: 6.2ft
Vertical obstacle ability: 24in.
Fording depth: 40in.
Ground clearance: 17in.
Turning radius: 37ft (twice its length)

This photo clearly shows the Lee modification to the M3 with the commander's machine gun cupola on the top of the turret. (IWM E14050)

THE M3 IN COMMONWEALTH SERVICE

In June 1940 the British Tank Commission arrived in the United States with hopes of contracting American factories to produce standard British tanks. However, the National Defense Advisory Board could not allocate production lines to produce entirely different models of tanks. All production lines were to be utilized to build tank designs adopted by the US Army. A percentage of these could be transferred to the British with reasonable requested modifications under Lend-Lease.

The British would be supplied with US M3s to be known as "Lees" and the modified versions known as "Grants." The main modification was a completely redesigned cast 37mm turret. While retaining the original turret ring, it was distinctly wider with a conspicuous rear bulge. Also, the No. 19 wireless set was mounted in the rear turret bulge to be operated by the commander or loader, eliminating the need for the wireless operator and reducing the crew to six. The modification replaced the cupola and its machine gun with a split hatch with a periscope in an effort to lower the profile. However, it was only a few inches lower. It added a pistol port to the left front quadrant. A 2in. Mk I smoke bomb thrower was mounted in the right front of the turret at a 35-degree angle. The final modification was sand skirts. Some 1,600 Grants were produced with the British turret on the M3 (Grant I), M3A2 (Grant III), M3A3 (Grant VII), and M3A5 (Grant IX).

The British designated the Grant I through IX and the US versions as the Lee I through IX. Some of these models were never built; they were simply assigned designations in anticipation of models that might be produced, such as the Lee IV, a hypothetical M3 with a diesel engine. Others, like the Lee III (M3A2), were never delivered to the British. Almost 200 Grants had been supplied to the British

A PzKpfw III Ausf L with a long 5cm gun. The pistol ports on the forward sides of the turret have been eliminated. The mounting bracket for the three-tube smoke candle projector devices (*Nebelkerze Werfergerät*) can be seen above the "7." They projected 92mm smoke canisters about 25m.

in time for the May 1942 Gazala battle. They saw their first action on May 27, 1942, at Bir Hacheim. In his memoirs, Rommel mentions, "There was also a British surprise awaiting us here, one that was not to our advantage – the new Grant tank. The advent of the new American tank had torn holes in our ranks." Some 600 had been delivered before the October El Alamein breakout. Eventually the Grants/Lees were replaced by M4s, but some were modified into command vehicles and other special purpose types. Others were shipped to India, and both Grants and Lees fought in Burma. A total of 757 Grants and Lees were provided to Australian units, but only a few saw action, on Borneo in 1945. In all, 2,855 Grants and Lees were provided to the Commonwealth between 1941 and 1943.

M3 SUPPORT ROLES

The M3 chassis and the tank itself, albeit much modified, served in numerous support roles. The chassis and lower hull was incorporated into the M4 Sherman tanks, the 105mm M7 and M7B1 Priest self-propelled howitzers, and the 155mm M12 self-propelled gun. The Canadian Ram I and II cruiser tanks were derived from the M3 as was the Kangaroo armored personnel carrier and the 25-pdr Sexton self-propelled howitzer. There were 805 M3-series tanks modified to serve on as M31 tank recovery vehicles. A 60,000lb capacity winch was installed inside the hull, and a boom crane was mounted on the rear deck. Armament was two .30cal machine guns with dummy 75mm and 37mm guns installed. The M31 was a modified M3 tank, the M31B1 from an M3A3, and the M31B2 from the M3A5. The British and Americans modified many as canal defense lights (CDL system intended to blind enemy gunners), Grant Scorpion III mine flail tanks, and command vehicles.

PZKPFW III AUSF L LIGHT TANK

German records are unclear as to the exact number of PzKpfw III variants in Tunisia, often simply listing them according to whether they had long or short 5cm guns. Owing to earlier losses most replacement PzKpfw IIIs were the Ausf J and L. Differences between the two were minimal and the Ausf L is discussed here as being the most representative. The Ausf L armed with a 5cm gun was the tenth PzKpfw III model produced. Production began in July 1942. It was almost identical to the much more numerous Ausf J. The only external differences were that extra spaced armor was added to the gun mantlet and the stepped front of the hull plus the forward side vision ports were removed. Some early production Ls retained these using Ausf J turrets. The add-on armor upped its weight from the Ausf J's 21.5 tons to 22.7. The first models weighed in at 19.5 tons, but each subsequent version's weight increased.

1. 5cm KWK 39 L/60 gun
2. Gun mantlet with add-on spaced armor shield
3. 5cm gun trunnion
4. Gun traverse handwheel
5. Turret air ventilator
6. Gun shield
7. Cupola vision blocks (x 5)
8. Turret escape hatch with pistol port
9. Commander's cupola with hatch
10. Pistol port
11. Add-on equipment bin
12. Commander's seat and bracket

PZKPFW III

Like the later Ausf J, the L mounted the long 5cm gun. Its gun sight was the TZf 5e. The bow machine gun was mounted in the *Kugelblende* (ballmount) *50*, and the driver was provided an improved armored *Fahrersehklappe* (driver's shutter) *50* with *Fahroptik* (driver's optics) *2*. *Gepack Kasten* (equipment storage bins) were fitted to the turret's rear from the Ausf J, which tankers called an *Essgeschirr* (owing its similarity to a mess kit).

The Germans used homogeneous armor on most of the tank, but the frontal armor was tougher to penetrate. *Zusatzpanzerung* (add-on armor protection) was gradually increased. The 30mm armor plates were bolted to the upper and lower nose of the Ausf H and some had spaced armor retrofitted. With the Ausf J the frontal armor was increased from 30mm to 50mm on the hull front. Spaced armor was added to the driver's compartment front step and to the gun mantlet beginning with the Ausf J. This was 20mm thick and intended to help defeat shaped-charge projectiles. The more common model in Tunisia was the Ausf L(tp) *(tropisch)* modified for desert use. It incorporated larger Fiefel air and oil filters; a single engine access hatch with air vents instead of two-piece, larger fan access doors; some pistol ports deleted; and improved crew compartment air circulation.

SPECIFICATIONS: PZKPFW III AUSF L LIGHT TANK

General
Production run: March 1941–late 1942
Vehicles produced: 1,549 (5cm L/42); 1,067 (5cm L/60)
Combat weight: 21,500kg (47,400lb)
Crew: Five (commander, gunner, loader, driver, radio operator)

Dimensions
Hull length: 556cm (116.1in.)
Width: 295cm (116.1in.)
Height: 250cm (98.4in.)
Ground contact length: 286cm (112.6in.)

Armor
Hull front: 5cm (2in.)
Hull sides: 3cm (1.2in.)
Hull rear: 5cm (2in.)
Hull roof: 1.6cm (.63in.)
Hull bottom: 1.5cm (.60in.)
Turret front: 5cm (2in.)
Turret sides: 3cm (1.2in.)
Turret rear: 3cm (1.2in.)
Turret roof: 1cm (.40in.)

Armament
Main gun: 5cm KwK 38 L/42 *kurz* or KwK 39 L/60 *lang*
Machine guns: 2x 7.9mm MG.34
Main gun rate of fire: 10–15 rpm

Ammunition storage
Main gun: 99 rounds (KwK 38 L/42); 84 rounds (KwK 39 L/60)
Machine gun: 3,750 rounds

Communications
Fu 5 receiver/transmitter

Motive power
Engine: Maybach HL120TRM
Power: 300hp at 3,000rpm
Fuel capacity: 320 liters (85gal)

Performance
Maximum road speed: 40k/hr (25mph)
Operational range: 145km (90mi)
Trench crossing ability: 200cm (79in.)
Vertical obstacle ability: 60cm (23in.)
Fording depth: 80cm (31in.)
Ground clearance: 38.5cm (15.2in.)
Turning radius: 5.85cm (19.2ft)

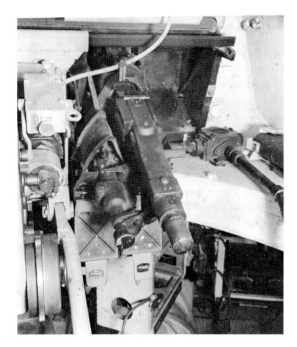

The view of a loader's position in an Ausf J PzKpw III. (Martin Windrow)

The 3.7cm *Kampfwagenkanone* 36 L/45 (KwK 36 battle vehicle cannon, or tank gun) was a derivative of the Rhinemetall-Borsig A.G. 3.7cm Pak 35/36 anti-armor gun. Development had begun in 1925, and it saw its first use in Spain in 1936. Considered at the time as one of the best antitank guns in the world, it was license built by the USSR, Italy, and the Netherlands and was purchased by China. By 1941 any 37mm gun was obsolete. KwK 36 was essentially the infantry gun modified to fit in a tank mantlet. It had the same semi-automatic loading features as the US M6 with a horizontally opening breechblock. Turret rotation and elevation were manual. Its maximum elevation was +20 degrees and depression -10. The gun was fired by a solenoid trigger from the gunner or commander's station, but the loader could fire it with an alternate trigger on the breech ring.

The 5cm *Kampfwagenkanone* 38 L/42 (KwK 38) was another Rhinemetall-Borsig design and was based on the Pak 38 towed antitank gun, but with about one-third of its length shorter barrel. Design of the Pak 38 began in 1936. It was essentially a scaled up 3.7cm Pak 35/36. The long 5cm KwK 37 L/60 began to be mounted on PzKpfw III Ausf Js in 1942. This was a purpose-designed tank gun of somewhat different design. It had a vertical breechblock and used a much larger cartridge case than the KwK 38. The 5cm guns had a 10–15 rpm rate of fire.

Many *Panzermanner* preferred the PzKpfw III over the PzKpfw IV owing to its higher speed. They both used the same engine. With the long 5cm gun they thought it a capable weapon against most Allied tanks. The PzKpfw IV's long 7.5cm was preferred by other tankers as it was a real killer even if the tank was slightly slower and had no more armor than its lighter brother. These tanks lacked gyrostabilized guns and had to halt to fire accurately.

PZKPFW III SUPPORT ROLES

The PzKpfw III chassis served as the basis for a number of specialized AFVs. Standard tanks were modified to become *Panzerbefehlswagen* (command vehicles) and *Panzerbeobachtungswagen* (artillery observation vehicles), both with the main gun removed and a dummy installed. Turretless tanks were outfitted as *Bergepanzerwagen* (recovery vehicles) and *Schlepper* (supply carriers). A version capable of driving underwater, the *Tauchpanzer* (diving tank), was supplied air via a snorkel hose. There was also a *Flammpanzer* (flame tank), mounting a flame gun in place of the main gun. The most important variant was the Sturmgeschultz III (Stug III). This was a PzKpfw III chassis with a low, sloped superstructure housing a 7.5cm gun or howitzer or 10.5cm howitzer in the bow as an assault gun. Extremely successful in both offensive and defensive roles, some 10,500 Stugs were produced.

THE COMBATANTS

TRAINING

US TRAINING AND TANKERS' DUTIES

If there was a common characteristic among tank crew training of any army it was the recognition of the absolute necessity of developing teamwork and speed. A well-coordinated, smoothly functioning crew was essential for survival and the ability to defeat enemy tanks and antitank guns. A crew required a multitude of skills in gunnery, communications, maintenance, repairs, rough terrain driving, observation, detecting targets, land navigation, and route selection, among others.

Inducted American soldiers were given aptitude tests to determine their technical abilities

41

and other skills. Those who demonstrated or were assessed to possess mechanical skills were sent into one of the many mechanic training courses. Such skills were also necessary for tankers. Unlike many less industrialized nations, American boys often had some degree of exposure to driving cars or at least farm tractors, and it was not uncommon for boys to tinker with the family car or even their own. Boys were also exposed to books and magazines that provided plans for hobby projects ranging from building radios to building simple mechanical devices. After induction, classification clerks reviewed the recruit's records and test results and often personally interviewed them.

Basic training may have taken place on any of numerous posts across the country, and future tankers were sent to Ft Knox, Kentucky, the Armor School south of Louisville. The new Armored Force was established in July 1940 along with the 1st Armored Division. The Armored Force School and Armored Force Replacement Training Center were organized in October. At that time, the Armored Force was not a formal branch of service like the infantry and artillery. It did have its own "branch of service" insignia, displaying a World War I Mk VIII tank. Its branch colors were green and white. Armored Force units were more readily identified by their triangular shoulder patch displaying the blue, yellow, and red of the infantry, cavalry, and artillery.

Tank crews in training in England in 1942 prior to their deployment to North Africa the following year. (CORBIS HU 047915)

A typical Panzer III crew in tropical shirts and shorts though the pith helmet would have been captured from some South African forces.

Individuals undertook specialty training and were then assigned to units, or specialty training may have been undertaken in the unit. Ideally basic was 13 weeks, but this was sometimes cut short. The initial basic training phase covered common skills to include dismounted drill, guard duty, small arms firing and qualification, bayonet, customs and courtesies, map reading, chemical defense, first aid, and field sanitation, among other skills taught to any other soldier. Often they were allowed to select their specific crew position on the tank. Gunners and assistants/loaders were assigned the specialty code "616," drivers "736," radio tender/gunners "776," and tank commanders "532" while platoon sergeants were "651." Once assigned to a unit and crews were formed, the soldiers received cross-training in one another's skills. This capitalized on the American qualities of initiative, teamwork, and the desire to get the job done with a minimum of interference from higher up.

The tank commander was responsible for everything his crew did or did not do. He oversaw its operation and maintenance and was responsible for the crew's discipline and well being. His station was in the cupola in the left side of the 37mm turret. The commander selected the tank's route, observed for enemy threats and obstacles, guided the driver, directed both gunners as to what targets to engage with what types of ammunition, gave the gunners firing orders, kept an eye on other tanks in the formation, ensured his tank maintained its position and ordered speed changes, and watched the platoon leader's tank to respond to its actions. All crewmen were interlinked by the intercom system.

The 75mm gunner and his assistant operated the main weapon, observed for targets, and followed the commander's firing orders. The 75mm gunner was second-in-command. The 37mm gunner and loader were stationed in the turret and also operated the coaxial machine gun. All gunners were responsible for the care and maintenance of all guns and ammunition. The driver or radio operator ran and maintained the radio and intercom system. The US used only voice radios and did not have Morse code capability, it being thought unnecessary for high-speed operations. The platoon commander's tank was equipped with an SCR (Signal Corps Radio)-528, a two-way FM radio with a range of 10–15 miles under ideal conditions, although a 5 mile-range was more realistic. The other four tanks had an SCR-538, which was a receiver only. The frequency range of both radios was 20–28 MHz, preventing them from netting with infantry radios. In a defensive position, wire was laid between the tanks for telephone communications. The driver steered the vehicle and had to be highly responsive to the commander's orders. Because the 75mm gun had only a limited traverse, the driver had to be alert to orient the tank, enabling targets to be engaged. This might have required sudden, major course changes and pivot turns to keep a moving target in the gun's limited field of fire. The driver also operated the fixed machine gun beside his station and was usually the third ranking crew member.

GERMAN TRAINING AND TANKERS' DUTIES

Prior to and early in the war, every German soldier undertook 16 weeks of infantry training. They could volunteer for the Panzerwaffe (Armor Force) and would be assigned if possessing a mechanical aptitude. In the new German Army the Panzertruppen were considered an elite arm and were provided with some of the most qualified and motivated young soldiers. The *Panzersoldaten* considered themselves bearers of the traditions of the Hussar, the old heavy cavalry. Training at the Panzertruppenschule at Wünsdorf south of Berlin was comprehensive and thorough. In January 1941 it was redesignated the Panzertruppenschule (Schule für Schnelle Truppen "Wünsdorf"). With the expansion of the Panzer-Divisionen, a second school was established in June 1941 from the old Cavalry School at Potsdam-Krampnitz southwest of Berlin as Schule für Schnelle Truppen "Krampnitz." In four months of

A Panzer III shown flying the Panzerwaffe's death's head insignia. This was common practice for command vehicles as displaying pennants eased identification on the battlefield. (Carlo Pecchi Collection)

instruction, all students were taught driver and maintenance skills as well as the basics of all crew functions. Many future *Panzermänner* had undertaken training in the National Socialist Motorized Corps (Nationalsozialistisches Kraftfahrrerkorps, the NSKK) where young men learned vehicle driving and maintenance skills. Many also served in the National Labor Service (Reichsarbeitsdienst), receiving premilitary training. Private ownership of automobiles was not widespread, and the NSKK served to familiarize members with motorized vehicles for employment in industry and the military. Gunnery was an important skill, and small unit tactics were incorporated into field exercises.

Enjoying a smoke alongside their PzKpfw III, this photo clearly illustrates the AfrikaKorps' relaxed attitude towards uniforms. (Carlo Pecchi Collection)

Prospective *Panzertruppen* officers and junior NCOs undertook special courses of instruction in which they also learned leadership, tactical and administrative skills, and political indoctrination. The highest qualities sought among *Panzermänner* were speed of action, resourcefulness, and cunning.

The Panzerwaffe had been established in July 1938 from the Kraftfahrkamptruppen (Motorized Battle Troops) and inherited that branch's pink arm of service color. They were better known by their black uniforms and the *Totenkopf* (death's head) collar insignia. The black wool uniform was replaced by reed-green tropical twill, but the Hussar death head insignia was retained. In September 1939 all armor, antitank, armor reconnaissance, motorized rifle, and motorcycle rifle units assigned to Panzer-Divisionen were consolidated with cavalry units to become the Schnelle Truppen (Mobile Troops). They would not be redesignated the Panzertruppen until March 1943.

Tank crewmen were selected for training in specific duty positions according to their demonstrated abilities early in training. Cross-training was not neglected. A German pamphlet captured in Libya outlines the duties of a *Panzeresatzung* (five-man tank crew):

The tank commander is an officer (platoon leader) or an NCO and is responsible for the vehicle and its crew. He indicates targets to the gunner, gives fire orders, and observes the effects. He keeps a constant watch for the enemy, observes the zone for which he is responsible, and watches for any orders from the commander's tank. In action he gives his orders by intercom to the driver and the radio operator and by speaking tube and touch signals to the gunner and loader. He receives orders by radio or flag, and reports to his commander by radio, signal pistol, or flags.

The gunner, a junior NCO, is the assistant tank commander. He fires the main gun, coaxial machine gun, or the submachine gun [for close-in defense] as ordered by the tank commander. He assists the tank commander with observation.

The veterans of the AfrikaKorps were noted for the effectiveness of its armor ambush (*Panzerwarte*). While Commonwealth forces had learned the hard way, the green Americans were vulnerable. There was no prescribed layout, it being dependent on available forces and weapons, the enemy formation and size, and, more than anything else, the terrain. Antitank guns would be positioned to achieve flank and rear shots after the enemy armor passed. The Panzers would not always remain in stationary positions but would engage from a hull delifade position (referred to as *Halbverdeckte* or *Randstellung*), opening fire from an unexpected direction and then maneuver to finish off or pursue the surviving enemy.

The loader loads and maintains the turret armament under the orders of the gunner. He is also responsible for the care of ammunition, and when the cupola is closed, gives any necessary flag signals. He replaces the radio operator if he becomes a casualty.

The driver operates the vehicle under the orders of the tank commander or in accordance with orders received by radio from the commander's vehicle. He assists with observation, reporting the presence of the enemy or obstacles. He watches gasoline consumption, reporting as it drops to specified levels, and is responsible to the tank commander for the care and maintenance of the vehicle.

The radio operator is under the orders of the tank commander. In action and when not actually transmitting, he always keeps his radio set to "receive." He operates the intercom system and records any important messages he may receive. He fires the bow machine gun. If the loader becomes a casualty he takes over his duties. [Tank radio operators were taught not to just operate the radio, but to make minor repairs and send and receive Morse code, though this was seldom used. The radio operator also carried a backup battery in case the tank lost its electrical power.]

All crewmen shared in maintenance and repair duties as well as servicing equipment and cleaning the tank's weapons.

Communications between tanks, subunits, higher units, and supporting arms was considered most critical by the *Panzertruppen*. While most armies installed only two-way radios in platoon commander's and higher echelon tanks, the Germans so

HAND SMOKE SIGNALS

Handrauchzeichen were small colored smoke cartridges thrown by hand onto the ground after igniting by a pull-cord friction igniter. They were mainly used to signal actions and events to supporting aircraft. They burned for 30–40 seconds and were distinguishable from 6,000ft (1,800m).

Color	Meaning
Orange	German troops here
Orange-red	We are isolated, cut-off, the enemy is behind us
Orange-green	Repeat your attack
Green	Increase range of action as we are advancing, we are attacking, or we are making contact
Red	The enemy is attacking [infiltrating, penetrating]
Red-green	The enemy is attacking [encircling] on our right
Red-white	The enemy is attacking [encircling] on our left
Violet	Enemy tanks ahead
Violet-red	Enemy tanks to our rear
Violet-green	Enemy tanks to our right
Violet-white	Enemy tanks to our left
Violet-orange	German tanks are going into action (to ensure aircraft did not attack them)

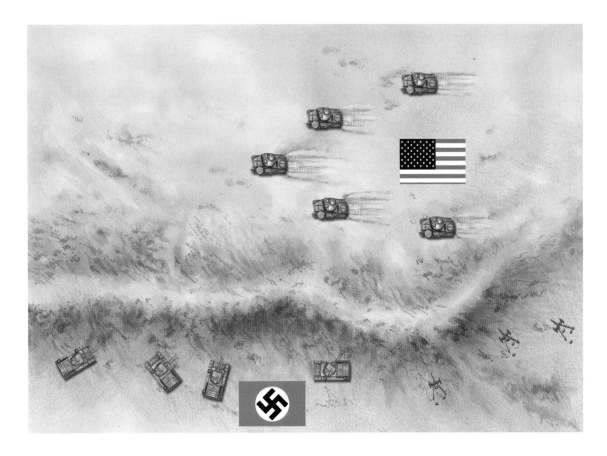

equipped all tanks in this fashion. Other armies held to the concept that tanks in the platoons were to only follow orders. It was thought that by eliminating two-way communications, response time would be speeded up. However, in reality this concept prevented subordinate tanks from achieving numerous tasks that included confirming the receipt of orders (or even that their radio was even operational), requesting a retransmission of orders drowned out by static or garbled transmissions, reporting they had successfully completed an action or were unable to, reporting detected threats to other tanks, adjusting supporting fires, reporting their fuel and ammunition status, or reporting they had mechanical problems. By allowing all tanks to transmit, the Germans were more responsive and able to pass information up the chain-of-command, which surely enhanced German combined arms tactics.

The Germans also considered two other means of communications: external (radio, flags, hand signals, flare pistol, flashlight, and hand smoke signals) and internal (intercommunication telephone, speaking tube, and touch signals).

Voice radio range between two moving tanks was about 6km (3.75 miles) in the desert and 10km (6.25 miles) using continuous wave (Morse code).

Flags were used for very short-range signaling and might not have been usable owing to dust, smoke, or fog. Signal flags were carried in holder tubes on the left of the driver's seat. When the cupola was open flag signals were given by the commander; when it was closed the loader raised the circular flap in the left of the turret roof and signaled through the port. Flag signals were given in accordance with a code, the meaning of any signal depending on the color of the flag (yellow, green, and red; US forces used the same colors) and whether the flag was held still or moved in a particular manner. Flags were soon discarded as being too conspicuous and were replaced by hand signals.

The 2.6cm flare pistol was used mainly to signal to accompanying infantry and artillery using colored smoke (during the day) and flares (at night).

The radio set, in conjunction with the intercom, provided the commander, radio operator, and driver with a means for external and internal voice communications.

Verbal orders were transmitted from the commander to the gunner by means of speaking tube and touch signals. The latter was also used for messages from the commander to the loader and between the gunner and loader.

Most German *Panzermänner* in Tunisia were battle-hardened veterans with many having been in Africa fighting capable Commonwealth forces for almost two years. Many had previously fought in Poland, the Low Countries, and France. The 10. Panzer-Division, while arriving in Tunisia only three months before Kasserine Pass, was a well-blooded division having fought in Poland, France, and Russia. They possessed what was called *kampfgeist* (battle spirit), demonstrating high morale, a sense of absolute duty, and obedience. These veterans diffidently rated the informal title of *Panzerfuchs* (armor fox), an experienced tanker.

An M3 crew in North Africa prepares for the day's operations. Maps can be seen on spread on the ground. Dress is rather informal. The shoulder guard of the 75mm gun can be seen though the side escape hatch.

UNIT ORGANIZATION

US ORGANIZATION

Only half of the 1st US Armored Division, Combat Command B (CCB), was initially deployed to North Africa. The rest of the Division arrived on December 22, 1942. These units did not fight as pure battalions but were instead organized into combined arms task forces. At this time, 1st Armored Division task forces were called "combat commands" designated CCA though CCD.[6] An armored regiment consisted of two medium (2d and 3d) and one light (1st) tank battalions with headquarters, reconnaissance, maintenance, and service companies plus a medical detachment. A medium tank battalion was organized into a headquarters company and three tank companies. Of the 1st Armored Division's four medium tank battalions three were equipped with M4s and M4A1s. The 2d Battalion, 13th Armored Regiment was equipped with M3 mediums. By the time of the Kasserine battles, many M3s had been destroyed, disabled, or broken down and were replaced by M4/M4A1s, although some M3s remained. The battalion suffered such high losses at Kasserine that M3 reserve stocks replaced its losses, and it had more M3s after the battles than before, and the 3d Battalion had even more. The 751st Tank Battalion attached to the 34th Infantry Division also used M3s in Tunisia.

Water in the desert was critical commodity. A binocular case is seen under this man's right arm.

The full strength medium tank company contained five officers and 144 enlisted men. The company headquarters section (one captain, 24 enlisted) had a ¼-ton radio jeep, an M2 command halftrack, and two M3 medium tanks, one for the CO and the other in reserve. The 18-man administrative, mess, and supply section had three 2½-ton cargo trucks to haul supplies, unit equipment, and kitchen gear. It also had an M6 tank destroyer (a ¾-ton truck mounting a 37mm antitank gun) for rear echelon defense. The maintenance section was headed by a lieutenant executive officer (XO, the second-in-command) with 15 enlisted men with two M3 halftracks and a jeep. The 1st–3d Tank Platoons were manned by a lieutenant and 29 enlisted. Platoons operated in two sections, one of three tanks under the platoon commander in No. 1 tank and the other two under the platoon sergeant, a staff sergeant, in the No. 4 tank.

A seven-man crew consisted of the tank commander, a sergeant (unless the platoon commander or sergeant); a 75mm gunner (corporal), a driver (technician 4 or 5), a

---

6   These were temporary task forces unlike the later "command commands" incorporated into the armored division organization.

radio tender/gunner (commonly called a "radio operator," a technician 4 or 5), a 37mm gunner (pfc), and two assistant gunners (pfc). The later six-man crew lost the radio operator, whose duties were assumed by the driver. All crewmen were armed with Colt .45cal M1911A1 pistols, and a Thompson .45cal M1928A1 submachine gun was also carried.

GERMAN ORGANIZATION

The one Panzer-Regiment of a Panzer-Division had two battalions, Panzer-Abteilung I and II, organized into a *Stabs-Kompanie* (staff company), two or three PzKpfw III and one PzKpfw IV *Panzer-Kompanien* (armor companies), and a *Panzer-Werkstatt-Kompanie* (armor workshop company). Until reinforcements began arriving after Operation *Torch,* the legendary armor units of the Afrikakorps consisted of only four tank battalions: two in each of Panzer-Regimenter 8 and 5 of the 15. and 21. Panzer-Divisionen. In the 10. Panzer-Division's Panzer-Regiment 7, the Kompanie 1 and 5 were the medium companies. Prior to Kasserine Pass the regiment fielded about 100 PzKpfw IIIs and 20 each IIs and IVs. The Germans formed *Kampfgruppen* of battalion and regimental size consisting of various mixes of tank, motorized rifle, motorcycle rifle, reconnaissance, antitank, and pioneer units tailored for specific missions and usually bearing the name of the commander.

The *leichte Panzerkompanie* (light armor company) consisted of four officers, 63 NCOs, and 91 enlisted men. The *Kompanietrupp* (company troop) was assigned two officers, six NCOs, and 21 enlisted men. Integral to this headquarters was a light tank platoon with five PzKpfw IIs for reconnaissance and two PzKpfw IIIs as a command tank and a spare. The *Kompanieführer* (company leader) was a Hauptmann (captain), but more typically an Oberleutnant (senior lieutenant). The second officer, a Leutnant, was the *Führer des Kompanies Trupps* overseeing the headquarters and trains. Three motorcycles were used by couriers, and a medium field car was used for headquarters equipment. The 1. to 3. *Zügen* (platoons; *Zug* singular) was manned by a Leutnant Zugführer, more often an NCO, 14 NCOs, and ten enlisted with five PzKpfw IIIs.

A five-man *Panzerbesatzung* included the *Panzerführer* (tank commander), *Richtschütze* (gun layer), *Kraftwagenfahrer für gepanzert Kraftwagen* (driver), *Funker für gepanzert Kraftwagen* (radio operator), and *Panzerschütze* (loader). The first three typically held the rank of Unteroffizier (corporal) or Unterfeldwebel (junior sergeant), with one per platoon being a Feldwebel (sergeant). The radio operator and loader were rated *Panzerschütze, Panzeroberschütze,* or one of the higher *Gefreiter* grades. All tankers were armed with a 9mm pistol, either a P.08 Luger or P.38 Walther. Each tank was provided a 9mm MP.40 machine pistol and a 2.6cm flare pistol.

The company was supported by a robust service organization of four elements, which in combat were placed under battalion control. The *Kraftfahrzeug Instandsetzungsgruppe* (motor vehicle maintenance squad) with three NCOs and 14 enlisted was transported by a light maintenance car, medium cargo truck, two SdKfz 10 light halftracks, and two motorcycles with sidecars. *Gefechtstroß I* (combat train I) was the supply and equipment repair element with seven NCOs and ten enlisted. This element had a Volkswagen field car and three medium cargo trucks, two for transporting fuel cans. *Gefechtstroß II* had four NCOs and 13 enlisted, 14 of whom were *Wechselbesatzung* (relief tank crewmen) with two medium trucks. The *Gepäcktroß* (baggage train) had one NCO and three enlisted with a medium cargo truck responsible for hauling individual clothing bags. Convalescing soldiers were often detailed to the *Troß* for light duty, the *Troßfrank* (train sick).

An M3 crewman takes care of a daily chore, swabbing out the main gun. A 4gal tin of oil is seen beside the 75mm M3 gun.

In Africa company organization was greatly streamlined. There were no spare tank crewmen, few trucks, and tanks were in short supply. The company troop's reconnaissance tanks were unavailable and tank platoons might have only three or four tanks, often of mixed models or even captured British tanks, including an occasional M3 medium.

DAILY LIFE

The routine duties of a tank crew, whether American or German, were similar. The crew dedicated a great deal of time to their tank. Oil, fuel, and air filters had to be constantly cleaned, especially important owing to the smothering dust. A clogged filter could quickly overheat and kill an engine. Track tension had to be checked and adjusted to prevent throwing a track at a critical moment. The radio operator spent a great deal of time cleaning and tinkering with the temperamental, fragile set. Heat and dust were its enemies, to say nothing of the rough ride and what this did to vacuum tubes (valves), condensers, soldered connections, and the delicate tuning.

Care of the armament was crucial. The main gun and machine guns demanded frequent cleaning, even without being fired. This also applied to optical sights and ammunition. Dusty ammunition coupled with oil and carbon buildup in machine guns jammed them. Dusty main gun cartridges might fail to extract. After repeated firing or cross-country travel, the main gun's recoil system had to be checked to ensure there was sufficient fluid in the recoil buffer, and the recuperator springs, which returned the gun to battery, had to be readjusted. Live firing of all weapons prior to combat was critical to zero them, that is, to ensure the sights were adjusted to coincide with the actual point of impact at set ranges. A good tank commander ran dry fire drills at every opportunity under varied conditions, including nighttime. Pistols and submachine guns had to be cleaned along with other crew kit, and a spare barrel for each machine gun had to be maintained.

Keeping the tank fed was an endless job. With an operating range of 120–200 miles, during high-tempo operations a tank had to be refueled every day or two, not so much because it actually traveled that distance, but because of the time it spent idling. Fueling was done by hand, and it was heavy work to boost 5-gal (20-liter) jerry cans up onto the hot engine deck and empty each into the filler tube. A full jerry can or *Benzinkanister* (fuel container) weighed 47–49lb. An M3 required 35 cans and a PzKpfw III required 16 to fill up. Fine cloth was placed over the filler hole to filter out dust and had to be cleaned between each can going in. Oil and transmission fluid had to be topped off and dozens of grease points, joints, and bearings squirted. Canteens and the water cask were filled regularly.

To restock a tank with ammunition was heavy work requiring the entire crew. The crated ammunition had to be unloaded from a truck, and the wooden boxes (metal in the case of the Germans) had to be opened, rounds had to be removed from sealed shipping tubes, and all of the packing materials had to be reloaded on trucks. Only in action were the packing materials discarded. Each round had to be passed up through the side escape hatches and individually stowed in cramped quarters. This might have to be accomplished during lulls in combat in order to cross-level ammunition between tanks. The Americans were fortunate in that machine gun ammunition was issued belted and tracers inserted. The 36 metal ammunition cans only had to be unpacked from wooden crates and stowed. The Germans received their ammunition loose in 1,500-round wooden boxes. The rounds had to be belted by hand in the nonexpendable belts, a tracer inserted every seventh round, the 150-round belts then correctly coiled into 25 canvas bags, and finally stowed.

A time held back in reserves allowed a crew to do all the vital maintenance to keep a tank running. Here the crew of an M3 prepare their tank for future combat in February 1943. (NARA)

Worn-out and damaged tracks had to be replaced, and this was a lengthy, labor-intensive job requiring all hands, as was replacing worn-out rubber-clad bogie wheels and return rollers. Spare sections of track links and bogie wheels were stowed on the hull as spares and for additional protection. As one tanker remarked, "Everything was so dang heavy."

Periodically, platoon and company commanders inspected the crews and machines. All work done on the tank had to be recorded in a log book (in German, *Fristenheft*). All necessary tools, crew and individual equipment, and spare parts were accounted for. Equipment included shovels, picks, axes, pry bars, jack, wire cutter, track tension tool, normal mechanic's tools, tow cable, fire extinguishers, camouflage net, first aid kit, flashlights, binoculars, and compass.

The infantry may have been jealous of tankers riding into battle, but it was hot, heavy, demanding work to keep their machines going.

Spare parts shortages were common on both sides. As a result, it was critical to recover conked-out or damaged tanks and to place them back in action or cannibalize them for parts. More often than not a knocked-out tank, what the Germans called a *Panzerleiche* (armor corpse), could be returned to action in short time.

Tankers may have ridden, but they did not ride in comfort. Even on sand roads, much less cross-country, it was a jolting experience riding on seats with minimal padding. Gun sight rubber eye and forehead protectors produced black eyes and bruises. The desert heat, easily in excess of 110°F (43°C), was one thing, but the inside of a tank frequently reached 120°F (49°C), and that was with all hatches open and the tank moving. Dust flooded through hatches, and the crew members who could, sat in the hatches. The driver though was confined inside, and with his hatch open he faced a full blast of dust from leading vehicles. As one American tanker recorded, "The dust was the worst part of it; that and the flies." The PzKpfw III was even driven with the break service hatches open to ventilate the front compartment. Going into combat, a tank had to shut all hatches, although the commander normally only closed his when absolutely necessary in order to effectively observe and be aware of the developing situation and terrain. A buttoned-up tank could heat up to over 130°F (38°C) with little air circulation. The engine and transmission generated more heat as did weapons firing. Propellant fumes from the main gun when it ejected cases and from the machine guns flooded the interior, already ripe with the smell of gasoline fumes, oil, sweat, and urine. Owing to the high-powered engine, the running gear, and grinding treads, the ride was incredibly noisy, whether the hatches were open or not. Intercom or speaking tubes had to be used to communicate with the man at one's shoulder.

A buttoned-up tank offered only very limited observation through vision slits, ports, periscopes, and gun sights, all with narrow fields of observation. There were many blind areas around tanks; obstacles and attacking infantry could not be seen if near the tank. Dust and smoke all but blinded a buttoned-up tank. The low silhouette PzKpfw III offered foreshortened observation, but the high-topped M3, with the commander's head 10ft above the ground when buttoned up, provided a good, though conspicuous vantage point. Yet he was so much higher than the driver and gunner that he had a different perspective of the action that they could not see.

In combat, crewmen relieved themselves into a can, bottle, or empty main gun cartridge case to be emptied out of the escape hatch, although spilled contents were a regular and unfortunate occurrence. American tankers had the advantage of being able to urinate or defecate into a machine gun ammunition can, which had an airtight sealable lid. It was tossed out, possibly to be recovered by an infantryman thinking he had found discarded ammunition.

A tank crew could carry a couple of days' rations along with cooking gear. By punching a hole in a ration tin, it could be heated on an exhaust manifold. An American crew carried a small M1941 one-burner gasoline stove. The Germans had similar stoves but more often used their little *esbit* cookers heated by fuel tablets. Another means of cooking was to fill a large ration tin half full of sand and soak it with gasoline. The sand prolonged the burn while an open ration can or mess kit was heated over it. And yes, an egg, when purchased from an Arab, could be fired on the engine deck with a dash of cooking oil.

The Americans were issued the infamous K-rations – three one-meal packets with small tins of mixed meat and vegetables, cheese spread, and crackers. An equally unpopular C-ration carton contained three larger tins of meat and vegetables and three more with crackers, spread, and instant coffee, providing three meals. They were also issued British "combo" (composite) ration packs with enough prepared and tinned foods for 14 men for one day. Emergency rations were the D-ration, a 4oz enriched chocolate bar intentionally made to taste like boiled potatoes to discourage snacking.

The Germans issued few prepackaged rations, but rather tinned sausage, meat spread, or sardines; compressed dried beans and peas; black bread from field bakeries or packaged preserved bread; tubes of cheese; ersatz coffee; and Italian tinned meat and hardtack, neither of which was popular. Rations were issued on a daily basis, and crews cooked them collectively, although an effort was made to serve a hot soup or stew meal once a day from the battalion kitchen. Fresh foods were seldom issued, but some were procured from Italian sources such as onions, olive oil, and marmalade. A 100-gram (3.5oz) chocolate disc *(Scho-ka-kola)* in a tin or fiberboard container was issued as emergency rations and was quite tasty. Captured British and American rations were highly valued.

Sleeping arrangements on both sides were similar. The Americans used shelter-halves, of which two were buttoned together to form two-man pup tents. The Germans used triangular-shaped shelter-quarters also worn as rain capes. Four could be buttoned together to make a pyramid-shaped, four-man tent. Often the shelter-halves or shelter-quarters were pitched as an awning, tied along the downwind side of

Panzer III crewmen relax outside their tank while one crew member receives a battlefield haircut. (Private collection)

the tank's track guard and the lower edge stacked to the ground. This was also done when sleep could be caught during the day, although the awning was pitched on the shady side. When shelter was unnecessary, tankers often bedded down at the rear of the tank to capture radiating engine heat. Desert nights were extremely cold. Troops bundled up in overcoats and wool blankets with two often used for insulation from the cold ground. The gasoline-rich Americans were known to splash fuel on the ground, light it, and wait for it to burn out before throwing their bedrolls over the warmed ground. Near the front, slit trenches were dug in which to sleep. In some instances a shallow pit was dug to the length and inside width of the tracks and the tank parked over it, providing the crew overhead cover. In bivouacs or laagers in forward areas, tanks and other AFVs parked facing outward in an all-around perimeter. If the ground was broken or wadis were present, the tanks positioned themselves in hull defilade. One crewman manned the turret, usually pulling one- or two-hour shifts. During lulls in action crews simply slept the best they could in their stations; again, at least one man remained awake.

The Germans issued Benzedrine, also known as Pervitin or Isophan, a methamphetamine and known today as "speed," to keep them alert and awake during prolonged combat. The bottles were marked only as "*Stimulant*" and with the directions "1 or 2 [5mg] only as needed to maintain sleeplessness." In 1941 German reports were enthusiastic of its use, but by the year's end they were more cautious, and in early 1942, warnings were issued. While reducing the desire for sleep, the resulting fatigue led to loss of efficiency and difficulty in accomplishing complicated tasks. It was directed that the drug's use would be confined to emergencies and not taken routinely. It was to be given only if there was a reasonable expectation that the crisis would end within 12 hours. Pervitin would not be given indiscriminately to large bodies of troops nor given to those whose duties required difficult decisions. It was to be administered under the control of a medical officer. Nonetheless there were soldiers who became addicted to *Stimulant*.

Lack of water was also a constant problem. There was seldom enough for drinking, much less for washing and shaving. Fortunately, tanks used air-cooled engines. The long-term result of doing with less water was gradual dehydration, headaches, lightheadedness, muscle and joint aches, weight loss, and high blood pressure. The worst effect of water deprivation is that blood volume is reduced and one's blood thickens. When wounded and succumbing to shock, blood vessels contract and the thickened blood aggravates the effects of shock.

Combat was unnerving, fast paced, confusing, and highly stressful. Sleep was infrequent and meals irregular. While comparatively immune to small arms and mortar fire and all but a direct artillery hit, there were many lethal threats to the tankers and their tanks. More tanks were lost to antitank mines than any other single cause. Antitank guns, tank destroyers, and other tanks were deadly. The 37mm and smaller caliber weapons caused little damage, but larger weapons could be fatal. The Germans feared the Matilda: even though it had only a 2-pdr (40mm) gun; it was nonetheless lethal. This resulted in add-on armor on the bow and gun mantlet. The American 75mm gun on the M3 medium tank and the M3 halftrack tank destroyer

The driver's compartment inside the British M3 Grant. The interior of the M3 Lee would have been virtually identical. It was remarkably spacious due to the atypical hull design. Note in particular the large open front visor. However, this let in blowing sand when on the move and would have to be closed. Thus when the tank was in action the driver's only view would be through the tiny slit to his left. (Tank Museum 2729/E2)

was lethal to every German tank in the theater, except the few late-arriving Tigers. For the Americans the short 5cm was dangerous, but the long 5cm was especially deadly. The Germans also mounted their own 7.5cm and captured Russian 76mm antitank guns on self-propelled mounts, and these were extremely lethal.

One of the hardest-working crewmen was the loader. In heavily gunned tanks hefting the rounds was indeed strenuous work. It was not so difficult for the light 37mm/3.7cm and 5cm guns, but still he had to work in cramped quarters retrieving rounds from difficult-to-access locations about the tank. He also had to avoid the gun's recoil and watch out for ejected cases. Loaders also re-stowed spent cartridges or tossed them from an escape hatch and shifted rounds from less accessible stowage to more rapidly accessed racks.

The driver was another hard worker. He steered using two hand-operated breaking/steering levers plus had to manually shift gears with a hand lever and clutch pedal. Additionally, there was the usual strain of driving, observing, and paying attention to the commander's "backseat driving." Good drivers steered their own course, seeking cover and clear routes. During motor marches to the front and even during combat, other crewmen might relieve the driver. Often drivers were spared watch duty to ensure their rest.

The radio operator, because of his relatively easy job, often accepted other duties such as preparing meals and looking after the quarters. The Germans called him a *Stullenmax* (untranslatable, but equating to "gofer").

Tank crews developed close bonds owing to the shared experiences of intense training and combat. They learned one another's strengths and weaknesses, who would cheer them up in bad times, and who pulled through no matter what the circumstances. The Americans simply called this teamwork; the Germans called it *Kameradschaft* (comradeship), having a deeply serious meaning when strong bonds developed between men who fought together.

COMBAT

The night of February 13, 1943, was cold, with the Sidi Bou Zid plain bathed in bright moonlight. General Eisenhower visited the 1st Armored Division CP outside of Sbeïtla over 20 miles northwest of Sidi Bou Zid. He then went on to Sidi Bou Zid, arriving at 0100hrs. Even though warnings had been issued to expect only diversionary attacks from Faïd Pass or the passes to the north and south, it was apparent to the troops that an attack was imminent. Regardless, the troops displayed little motivation, and defensive preparations were poor. German activity had been increasing, and there was a great deal of troop and vehicle movement. It was pointed out that the US infantry defending the high ground were extremely exposed. While they occupied good observation positions, they could be easily cut off and become unable to contribute to the battle on the plain. The 3d Battalion, 1st Armored Regiment in Sidi Bou Zid, reinforced by a dozen halftrack tank destroyers, was down to 40 M4 tanks. A battalion of self-propelled 105mm howitzers and another of towed 155mm howitzers were positioned to the rear. The trains had withdrawn for the night. CCC, serving as a mobile reserve, was located near Hadjeb-el-Aïoun 12 miles north of Djebel Lessouda. Task Force Kern was 40 miles away near Sbeïtla as the division reserve. The Germans were expected to have air superiority, and they had good observation of the area from the higher ground they held to the east.

The American tankers just to the west of Sidi Bou Zid were coiled up in a laager for all-around defense. They were to be on full alert, although crewmen took turns dozing. The infantrymen in the hills were also on full alert in their slit trenches and sangars. The infantry were nonmotorized, being attached from the 34th Infantry Division. They hadn't erected any barbed wire nor laid any minefields other than a small one off the east end of Djebel Ksaira. The stiff wind blew up an early morning sandstorm and carried the sounds of tank engines and tracks, but the distance and direction could not be determined.

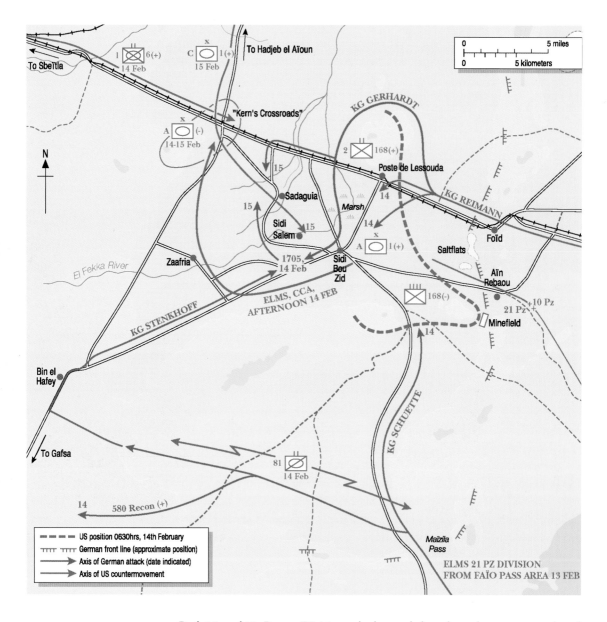

The following labels appear on the map:

To Sbeïtla

1 ⊠ 6(+)
14 Feb

C ⬭ 1(+)
15 Feb

To Hadjeb el Aïoun

"Kern's Crossroads"

KG GERHARDT

A ⬭ (-)
14-15 Feb

2 ⊠ 168(+)

Poste de Lessouda

KG REIMANN

N

15

Sadaguia

Marsh

Sidi Salem

15

14

14

A ⬭ 1(+)

Foïd

Saltflats

El Fekka River

Zaafria

1705,
14 Feb

Sidi Bou Zid

Aïn Rebaou

ELMS, CCA,
AFTERNOON 14 FEB

⊠ 168(-)

+10 Pz
21 Pz

Minefield

KG STENKHOFF

14

KG SCHUETTE

Bin el Hafey

To Gafsa

81 ⬭
14 Feb

14   580 Recon (+)

Maïzila Pass

ELMS 21 PZ DIVISION
FROM FAÏO PASS AREA 13 FEB

0   5 miles
0   5 kilometres

- - - - US position 0630hrs, 14th February
⊤⊤⊤⊤ German front line (approximate position)
⟶ Axis of German attack (date indicated)
⟶ Axis of US countermovement

The battle of Sid Bou Zid,
February 14–15, 1943

Both 10. and 21. Panzer-Divisionen had recently been brought up to strength and was well equipped with PzKpfw IIIs with long 5cm guns and PzKpfw IVs with the long 7.5cm. The 10th fielded 110 and the 21st 91 tanks, about two-thirds being PzKpfw IIIs. There was also a company of 12 new 8.8cm gun-armed PzKpfw V Tiger tanks. The tankers were a mix of long-term African veterans, veterans transferred from other theaters, and fresh replacements from training units.

The 1st Armored Division fielded 202 M4 and M3 medium tanks and 92 M3 and M5 light tanks plus considerably more halftracks, tank destroyers, self-propelled artillery, and scout cars than the Germans. The numerical superiority was negated owing to the tanks' and halftracks' lighter armor, lighter- and shorter-ranged guns, inexperience, and widely scattered deployment.

PANZEROBERSCHÜTZE BALDUR KÖHLER (1923–)

Baldur Köhler was born in Offenbách near Frankfurt. His father had a shop in which he sold small electrical appliances, and he trained his son to make repairs. When conscripted in March 1942, Baldur undertook training in a signals replacement unit as a radio repairman. He was posted to Panzer-Regiment 25, 7. Panzer-Division in June 1942. The division had just arrived from the Eastern Front and was rebuilding in France, the *Butterfront*, where food was plentiful and life easy. Upon arrival, much to his surprise, he was issued a black uniform and was given radio operator and Morse code training with a small group of men within the regiment. Köhler was unenthusiastic at first and had difficulties with the code, but when the men underwent machine gun training, he began to warm up to the idea. Once assigned to a tank crew he and the others undertook a great deal of crew and unit training. In November they participated in the occupation of southern France, but in December he was assigned to a march battalion for transport to North Africa. He did not realize it at the time, but he was already assigned to 10. Panzer-Division, itself in France, which was being sent to Africa. They traveled by rail to Italy where they were issued tropical uniforms and equipment. The next step was a trip to Sicily by ferry and then by landing barge to Tripoli in a frightening night run. Tank crews were formed from the arriving replacements to man repaired and recently delivered tanks. Their tank commander, who had just been released from convalescence leave, was a long-time veteran of Africa and taught them immeasurably valuable lessons. Their gunner had served on the Eastern Front, and they felt gifted to have his experience. The driver and loader had served only in the 7. Panzer-Division as had Köhler. They participated in a number of engagements in January prior to the Kasserine Pass battles. They had virtually no opportunities for unit training, but their commander seemed to know instinctively what to do. When asked if he had ever seen Rommel, Köhler said the highest ranking officer he ever saw was his regimental commander. Köhler has never made any effort to locate his former crew, and he has no idea what became of them. Kasserine was an exciting adventure for him, but he does not see himself as being part of an important historical event. It was just a place and situation to which fate had sent him. In the 1950s he became a civilian service group employee of the US Army and repaired radios for 26 years. (Pictured are the shoulder strap with the *Panzertruppe* pink branch of service color, the *Panzeroberschütze* insignia worn on the upper left sleeve, and the *Panzertruppe* death's head insignia worn on the lapels of tropical uniforms.)

The white-painted village of Sidi Bou Zid looking northeast. On the left edge of the plain is the area in which so many American tanks were destroyed on February 14–15, 1943.

The *Panzertruppen* of four *Kampfgruppen* had been briefed the night before, fuel was topped off, and all tanks carried extra ammunition that was stacked on the floor. The men were given a hot meal, and after dark, once the danger of air attack had passed, they formed up in assembly areas ready to quickly move into columns for the 10. Panzer-Division advance through Faïd village and the 21. Panzer-Division elements through Maïzila Pass from the south.

The American routine was to pull back into tight defensive positions at night and an hour before dawn, about 0500hrs, would fan out toward Faïd Pass with patrols sent out during the night. Once in position the Americans would breakfast on cold K-rations. At 0630hrs columns of Panzers emerged from Faïd Pass, advancing toward the American positions on Djebel Lessouda. The blowing sand made it impossible for American observers to accurately determine numbers.

When moving on roads, on which the initial advance was conducted, Panzer companies drove *reihe* (single file) or in a *doppelreihe* (double file). If attacking on a narrow front, they would form into a *keil* (wedge) with one platoon in the lead and

Shown during the initial stages of the fighting, a halftrack-mounted 105mm T19 howitzer moves forward at the western end of Kasserine Pass in an attempt to reinforce the exits from the valley. (NARA)

two back on line. The platoons themselves were either in a *keil* with the *Zugführer* at the point or in a *doppelreihe*. On a wider front two platoons would be forward and one to the rear, an inverted or broad wedge *(breitkeil)*, allowing the rear platoon to move to either flank. Commanders led from the front. The advance was slow, and once the sandstorm abated, the Germans continued at a slow speed. This prevented exact tank locations from being detected, raised less dust to obscure the vision of other tanks, made less noise, allowed accurate fire on the move, and conserved fuel. The Germans sometimes moved at such a slow pace that from a distance it appeared they were not moving and could only be determined to be doing so by comparing their locations to terrain features.

As the German formation advanced along the Faïd–Sbeïtla road running between the defended hills on either side, it deployed across wider frontages and split into smaller formations. Kampfgruppe Gerhardt swung to the north to loop around Djebel Lessouda. Kumpfgruppe Reimann split into two formations and turned southwest off the road and followed along a road to the southwest. Tanks of Company G, 3d Battalion, 1st Armored Regiment were in screening positions on the plain and were knocked out, including the command tank in communication with Lessouda Force. Visibility was such that the force on Djebel Lessouda could not see what was occurring on the plain. CCA dispatched Companies H and I, 1st Armored and part of Company A, 701st Tank Destroyer Battalion up the road from Sidi Bou Zid "to clear up the situation." The first of several German air attacks arrived at this time. While en route the force was warned from Lessouda that at least 20 Mk IVs were at Poste de Lessouda. The Americans were taken under 8.8cm or 7.5cm antitank gun fire and possibly by four Tigers. The long-range fire drove off the Americans, preventing them from assessing enemy strength and dispositions. No reports were received from Company G screening the plain, but the troops on Lessouda reported 80 AFVs and trucks moving to the hill from the north and that there were 39 Mk IVs and some Tigers on the west side. Most of the "Mk IVs" were in actuality probably PzKpfw IIIs. The enemy force was slowly moving south toward the main road and firing at US hill positions. A general withdrawal to the southwest was ordered at 1100hrs. Enemy forces were approaching Sidi Bou Zid from the northwest and southeast and were supported by air attacks from 1000 to 1100hrs.

As the attacks from Faïd were being launched, 21. Panzer-Division elements in the south rumbled through Maïzila Pass at 0600hrs. They experienced difficulties going on the soft sand road. American fighters strafed one column, and patrols screening to the south reported 20 unidentified vehicles with ten heading north and ten turning west. The lead elements of Kampfgruppe Schuette moving north to Djebel Garet Hadid were

A view of a Panzer III (probably Ausf N) abandoned in the El Guettar Valley in 1943. (Getty)

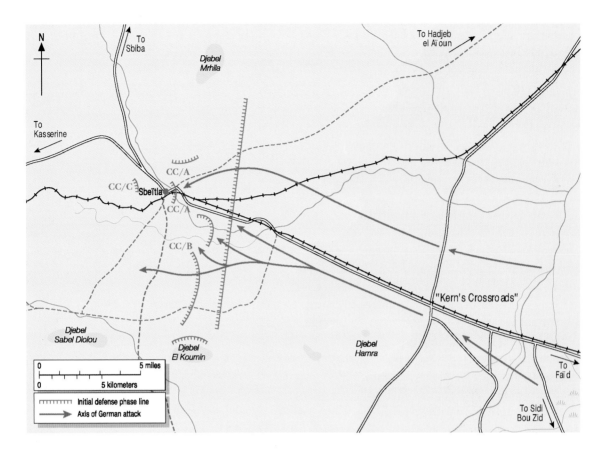

Inside the map:

N

To Sbiba

Djebel Mrhila

To Hadjeb el Aïoun

To Kasserine

CC/A

CC/C Sbeïtla

CC/A

CC/B

"Kern's Crossroads"

Djebel Sabel Diolou

Djebel El Koumin

Djebel Hamra

To Faïd

To Sidi Bou Zid

0   5 miles
0   5 kilometers

Initial defense phase line
Axis of German attack

Defense of Sbeïtla,
February 17, 1943.

engaged by the hill's defenders, and skirmishing took place through the afternoon. The battle group's main body arrived in the late afternoon to join the battle. Kampfgruppe Stenkhoff was experiencing difficulties moving cross-country westward to Bir el Hafey with vehicles mired in mud areas and experiencing mechanical breakdowns. It finally reached the town before 1600hrs, turned onto the road, and headed for Sidi Bou Zid, 18 miles to the northeast.

The 1st Armored Division's CP was receiving conflicting and incomplete reports. It was impossible to sort out the enemy situation because so many different groups of German vehicles were being reported in so many areas. Reports of Tigers resulted in most of an additional tank destroyer company being deployed along with a battery of self-propelled artillery. Concerns were heightened by noon when half of 3d Battalion, 1st Armored was reported destroyed, more accurate reports of the size of the German force south of Sidi Bou Zid were received, and it was realized that the forces on Djebel Lessouda and Djebel Ksaira were surrounded. Permission was granted in the early afternoon for the forces around Sidi Bou Zid to evacuate. Remaining American tanks were attempting to cover the withdrawal of CCA. Counterattacks were planned for the next morning to relieve the infantry stranded on the hills. Any daylight attempt for the foot-mobile hill forces to break out through German armor across the plain would have resulted in ground and air attack and heavy losses. Rommel said of the battle, "The Americans had as yet no practical battle experience, and it was now up

TECHNICIAN 5TH GRADE PAUL KIRBY (1921–)*

When the draft notice came in September 1941 Paul Kirby was more relieved than anything else. He knew it was only a matter of time before he was called, and now the suspense was over. Born in a small farming community west of St Louis, Missouri, he had no idea what he would be doing in the army. He was sent to Ft Knox, Kentucky, and assigned to the Armored Force Replacement Training Center where he underwent basic. He was then assigned to 2d Battalion, 13th Armored Regiment, 1st Armored Division. Kirby thinks he was assigned to armor because he had done a lot of tractor and dump truck driving. When thousands of American boys volunteered for service following the Pearl Harbor attack, Kirby felt like an old veteran. He was trained as a 75mm gun loader in an M3 medium tank because of his size, remarking, "Hay bales were a lot heavier than a seventy-five round." He had not participated in the prewar maneuvers, but within two months after assignment to the division, it was shipped by rail to Ft Dix, New Jersey, and then sea lifted to Northern Ireland. There he was reassigned as the 75mm gunner when an ejected cartridge case broke the gunner's wrist. After extensive training they staged to England then landed near Oran, Algeria, on November 8, 1942. Action was relatively light, but his group did a lot of driving to reach Tunisia. It was wearing on the tanks and crews. The food was poor, and the changing, harsh weather conditions wore them out

further. Their training had not prepared them for the conditions they faced. As a gunner Kirby credits himself for firing on and hitting four German tanks, all Mk IIIs, knocking out one. This was prior to the Kasserine battles. He thinks he hit an Italian light tank, but at least two other tanks or tank destroyers were firing on it so he is not certain if he even hit it, much less killed it. He had a great deal of respect for the Germans and knew they had considerably more experience than his unit, a fact that kept nagging at him though the campaign. "I frankly was afraid of them. They had been fighting the British for so long, and we were the new kids on the block." Kirby's only regret was that he could not return to farming in full capacity owing to a knee injury he sustained in battle. Instead he sold farm implements. One of his sons served in the army as an M48 Patton tank gunner in West Germany in the late 1960s. (Pictured are the Tech 5 rank insignia and the Armor Force collar insignia.)

* Tech 5 was equivalent to a corporal, but had no leadership responsibilities. "Paul Kirby" wishes to remain anonymous and has used the names of two former buddies.

to us to instill in them from the outset an inferiority complex of no mean order."

The 1st Battalion, 6th Armored Infantry and a light tank company were dispatched from the division reserve to a crossroads 11 miles northwest of the embattled town. This feature would become known as Kern's Crossroads, named after Commander Col William Kern, 6th Armored Infantry. Withdrawing CCA elements would reassemble behind this screen. Fleeing vehicles mired in soft sand and those that broke down were being abandoned as units withdrew under long-range artillery and tank fire. Surviving units would attempt to defend the route to Sbeïtla.

In the meantime the Germans continued to press in. Kampfgruppe Stenkhoff from the south linked up with 10. Panzer-Division elements west of Sidi Bou Zid at 1705hrs. Nightfall was fast approaching. General Ziegler determined at 1530hrs that the day's mission had been accomplished. The 10. Panzer-Division was directed to reconnoiter north to Hadjeb-el-Aïoun 25 miles to the north while 21. Panzer was ordered to assemble and be prepared by 1200hrs the next day for operations directed against Gafsa. There were still resolute American defenders on the bypassed hills, and no doubt an American counterattack was being planned. In order to meet this possibility, Ziegler did not disperse his forces too widely.

Panzeroberschütze Baldur Köhler was a *Funker für gepanzert Kraftwagen* (radio operator) of a PzKpfw III. Interestingly, he knew his tank only as a *"Panzer drei lang"* (Panzer three long), and he had no idea which variant it was. With a 5cm long gun it may have been an Ausf J, L, or M, but he was not familiar with the *Ausführung* term. He was assigned to Kompanie 5, Abteilung II, Panzer-Regiment 7, 10. Panzer-Division. On the morning of February 14, 1943, the troops were awake and manning their tanks hours before dawn. The evening before, they had cleaned the air filters and guns. Breakfast was preserved bread, marmalade, and ersatz coffee or tea. Knowing this was a major action, they were keyed up and confident not only in their years of experience, but also knowing that the Americans were inexperienced, slow to respond, and thinly spread. Their confidence was increased by their many recent small victories, and their commanders were plainly disdainful of the *Amis* (Americans). It was not without a sense of excitement that the *Panzermanner* sparked the electric primer igniters in their guns to test them, adjusted engine chokes, and pressed starter buttons. They started off at 0400hrs with a strong sandstorm blowing from the northwest – an excellent condition.

Moving slowly the Germans advanced along the Faïd–Sidi Bou Zid road. They had been briefed that there were some American tanks blocking the road between the hills on either side. The hills were held by American infantry. Köhler, manning his machine gun in the tank's bow, was surprised to see they were turning off the road and starting north on what appeared a route to attack Djebel Lessouda. He was concerned because tanks did not attack hills. He knew they were being followed by trucks of Panzergrenadier-Regiment 86. His tank commander reported other tanks were swinging to the south toward the town. It made sense now that they were going to cut off the enemy on the hill. The sandstorm abated, but a thick haze hung low of the plain. Slowly crawling across the broken ground, their turret traversed to the left and began cracking off occasional rounds at the hill. In return they received sporadic mortar rounds and inaccurate antitank fire. Even though the platoon leader occasionally sent instructions to fire on hillside targets over the radio he was manning, Köhler was no more aware of what was going on than anyone else in the tank. When German aircraft came over they would throw orange smoke signals out of the tank to identify themselves. Eventually they rounded the hill and found abandoned artillery positions, some still containing artillery pieces – even trucks and equipment had been left behind. The area appeared to have been heavily blasted by their artillery and bombs.

Reaching the road behind the hill again late in the morning they could see many columns of black smoke and clouds of dust in the direction of Sidi Bou Zid and to the south. Their force split yet again with part moving toward Sidi Bou Zid. They turned right on to the road and continued for several kilometers before turning on to a southbound road at which time they spread out into a broad wedge. They soon halted in a wadi with engines idling. They were in a *Beobachtungsstellung* – an observation position in which the commander's cupola was exposed over the lip of the wadi. The radio suddenly crackled a warning that American tanks were approaching from the northwest and that large clouds of dust were visible. The crew concluded that it must be a massive force to raise so much dust.

It was soon realized that the American M4 tanks were charging in a "V" formation across the plain toward Sidi Bou Zid. Their formation was scattered, and the dust they were raising was blinding the following tanks. German antitank guns concealed in an olive grove opened fire on the lead tanks. Word came over the radio to hold fire until ordered, then not to advance until ordered. The antitank guns continued to fire on the charging Americans. The Germans could admire their courage, but the tank commander, the only long-time African veteran among the crew, kept yelling how foolish they were. Shortly the platoon leader ordered his tanks to assume a *Feuerstellung* – a fire position in a *Halbverdeckte* or *Randstellung* (hull defilade). They knew they would soon be in action and that a *Panzerwarte* (armor ambush) was about to be executed against the exposed American flank.

With green flares arcing into the sky and the radio command *"Feuer!"* Köhler and the crew opened up at a rapid rate. The tank bucked slightly and dust leaped off the ground as rounds were pumped out and cartridge cases clanged in the turret. Seated in the hull with the tank squatting in a wadi, Köhler could see little and he felt helpless, that he was not even contributing to the fight. *"Anfahren!"* crackled over the radio, and the Panzers crawled out of the wadi, creeping slowly toward burning tanks. The Americans were running. Tanks and halftracks were pulling back. Some tanks were moving in reverse, attempting to cover others. Burning vehicles were scattered all about, some in clusters with their rear ends facing them. The gunner later said he had not seen anything like this since Russia.

The Germans pursued the Americans, threading their way through burning tanks and scattered bodies. They did not see any knocked-out Panzers. It was difficult to detect targets through the smoke and dust, and the Panzers crawled even slower. There were shouts over the radio that the *Amis* were getting away. It was then that the radio went dead, as did the intercom. The commander ducked down and yelled at Köhler, ordering him to fix it as though it was his fault. Köhler pulled out the radio from its case. It was so hot he could barely touch it. Nothing else was obviously wrong. They pulled up beside another tank so that it could be relayed to the platoon leader that they had lost their radio. In frustration

Köhler began machine-gunning abandoned American trucks, resulting in the commander yelling *"Feuerpause!"* ("Cease fire!"). The *Ami* trucks would be recovered for their own use.[7] Feeling worthless Köhler spotted movement behind a pile of rocks, and through drifting smoke he made out an antitank gun. He swung his machine gun and pressed on the trigger, hammering out a long thread of white tracers that ricocheted in all directions but peppering the gun shield. The commander yelled at him again, but then realized what Köhler's target was. The coaxial machine gun opened up, smothering the target in a shower of tracers as other Panzers joined in.

Köhler lost all track of time. His tank had halted, moved, halted again. At dusk they were ordered into a wadi to laager. It was not long before word spread that over 30 *Ami* tanks had been knocked out along with many halftracks and trucks. Their own losses were light. They did not expect a counterattack that night, and none materialized in the morning.

An American counterattack failed on the 15th, and during the night of the 16–17th, the infantry cut off on Djebel Ksaira and Garet Hadid were ordered to exfiltrate. Destroying heavy weapons and equipment, they struck across the plain 15 miles to Djebel Hamra. They were caught in the open at dawn by motorized units and

7 So many captured and recaptured trucks, British, American, German, Italian, and French (shipped from the Continent or bartered from the Vichy French), were used that tank columns approaching supply convoys could only identify them by their reaction, i.e., whether they continued on their course or scattered to evade.

PZKPFW III GUNNER'S VIEW

Range 200m: The 5dm gun has been fired and the tracer is en route to the halftrack driver's compartment

The round passes through the driver's compartment and explodes in the rear, igniting ammunition.

1,400 were captured. The Germans paused, and the 10. and 21. Panzer-Divisionen assembled in the Sidi Bou Zid area.

The 2d Battalion, 13th Armored Regiment, the most battle-experienced battalion in the 1st Armored Division, was not committed until the afternoon of February 17. The renewed German effort was directed at the south side of Sbeïtla held by CCB. The 2/13th Armor was at less than 50-percent strength, and while originally equipped solely with M3 mediums, now had some M4s and M4A1s in addition to over 20 M3s. The tanks were in serious need of maintenance, as the rubber track pads and bogie wheel and return roller rubber linings were severely chewed up after many miles of travel. The battalion was in defiladed positions some 4 miles southeast of the town. The 601st Tank Destroyer Battalion was outposted to the east, the 27th Armored Field Artillery Battalion backed the tankers, and two companies of 2d Battalion, 6th Armored Infantry were dug in on hills on either side of the road.

Technician 5th Grade Paul Kirby was his M3 tank's 75mm gunner. He should have been rated a corporal, but he was slotted as a driver on paper. It made no difference to him: both ranks drew the same pay. The crew had been together for over one year and rank meant nothing, so long as everyone knew Sergeant Henry was the man in charge. Henry ran a tight ship, but every man knew his job. It was seldom that Henry had to tell anyone what to do or when to do it.

The Americans had been rushed to the front amid wild rumors of a compete rout. The enemy was heading straight at them, and nothing had been able to stop the Germans.

FEBRUARY 18, 1943

A round is fired at the rear of the M3 detonating the engine compartment and blowing off the engine covers.

The gunner switches to the machine gun range scale to fire on any crewmen abandoning the M3.

There were rumors of just about every tank being knocked out and huge numbers of Americans taken prisoner. There was talk of Tiger tanks as well. During the march their tank had thrown a tread on a rough stretch of road, and it took hours to reinstall.

In darkness their tanks had maneuvered into a wadi. Ground guides walked ahead to ensure no stray troops were driven over or the tanks fell into a ravine. The Americans first found a position that allowed them to bring the 75mm gun to bear and then backed down the slope until only the 37mm turret peeked over the edge. The Germans owned the sky and camouflage was essential, but the Americans had difficulty erecting the camouflage net in the dark, which kept hanging up on the antenna, projections, and brush. They were good on ammunition and rations, but had little water. Sergeant Henry detailed sentries, an air guard to be posted at dawn, and two men for a water detail, if it was available from the company supply point. The men cleaned the guns and double-checked the troublesome turret control boxes. The Germans were expected to attack at dawn. No one got much sleep, and every man would be alert an hour before sunrise. No one had much appetite. Kirby could not even finish a 4oz D-ration bar.

The Germans did not attack at dawn but instead conducted probes to find passable terrain and to test the Americans. Just after noon, Jerry tanks and aircraft finally came in strength from the south and the infantry from the east. The Americans stowed the camouflage net in anticipation of having to move out. The tank destroyers bore the brunt of the attack, and many were knocked out. Others withdrew to alternate firing positions after firing smoke shells. The American defense was in-depth and well disposed in the wadis and dunes.

On the south flank the 2/13th Armor was well hidden. For once the Americans had an advantage. The main attack struck at 1315hrs with the Germans having to cross broken ground. Reports were of Mk IV tanks in superior numbers, but most were actually Mk IIIs.

Kirby could see the Panzers coming through his periscope, which was just high enough to see over the wadi's edge. His gun could not be brought to bear … yet. Jerry fighters streaked over, and the Panzers crawled in clear view toward the Americans. The firing order blared over the radio, and US guns began to crack, including their own 37mm, for what it was worth. The engine gunned and the tank jerked up the slope, bringing the "seventy-five" to bear. Kirby centered the statia lines on the bow of a Mk III and was about to punch the trigger when a tracer streaked into the German, kicking dust off it. The Panzer jerked to a stop. Kirby immediately traversed the gun to the right and aimed at another Panzer. It dropped into a wadi, and he anxiously waited for it to emerge. The knocked-out Panzer to the left suddenly began moving forward, traversing its long gun toward them.[8] Kirby shouted a warning over the intercom and was aware that the 37mm turret was turning. He fired at the second Panzer as it bounded out of the wadi and saw the tracer wang off the gun mantlet. The 37mm fired at the same time the German did. Kirby heard and felt two thumps. He guessed both German tanks had fired on them. There was a horrid clanging noise

---

8   It was a common German practice to halt and play dead when hit after a nonpenetrating shot and then return to "life."

above and behind him. Countless sparks showered and bounced out from under the turret shield, and Kirby immediately smelled smoke. The driver yelled to bail out, and Kirby struggled to climb over his seat. His loader dropped the round he held ready and ducked under the gun. Kirby saw a booted leg of one of the turret crew beneath the turret shield amid popping sparks. The fighting compartment was filling with thick, gray smoke. He slapped the side escape hatch lever and pushed it open. Air gushed in, and he heard a woof sound behind him and felt a heat blast. Kirby lost any sense of gallantry about letting the loader out first. He thrust himself through the hatch and fell face first on the rocks. The loader landed on him, knocking the breath out of both of them. The loader pulled Kirby to his feet, and they ran. Kirby remembered tank guns firing and artillery landing all around them. He did not know if it was American or German fire. Looking back he saw black smoke boiling out of the escape hatch. Then the turret blew off in an orange fireball.

The initial blast of American surprise fire knocked out at least five Panzers. American tank destroyers, pulling back to a rally point from which they were to reorganize and counterattack, came under heavy artillery fire, delaying their counterattack. Other vehicles were withdrawing, and many of the tank destroyers were caught up in the flow back to Kasserine. The Germans were quick to reorganize and again attacked the south flank. Battalion sent down the order to begin a phased withdrawal. Units began falling back to Kasserine, and defenses were established to the south and east.

Kirby and his loader were picked up by a tank destroyer. They said nothing about the rest of their crew. The two were dropped off at a fuel dump north of the road and detailed to help gas up tanks that started rolling in after nightfall (1900hrs). Word spread that at least nine tanks of the understrength unit had been lost. They stacked 5gal jerry cans on tanks and halftracks and caught another lift through Kasserine, ending up in a bivouac area for the night. There they found their driver who had been hit by spalling when a 5cm round struck beside his hatch. The driver was given to another tank to replace a wounded man, and they were assigned to a scratch crew for a previously mine-damaged M3.

All units were ordered to pull back to Tébessa and take up positions to the southeast along with retreating French colonial troops. Sbeïtla was under Allied air and artillery fire, key structures had been demolished, the water system destroyed, and mines were laid to hamper the Germans. US losses had been high, and morale was at an all-time low. But replacement troops, tanks, and vehicles were available, and most of the trains and support units had escaped to play a vital role in reconstituting battered units. The 21. Panzer-Division secured Sbeïtla, but 10. Panzer-Division was held back owing to a miscalculation of Allied strength, and thus the offensive tempo slowed. The fighting continued, and Rommel took Kasserine Pass on February 20.

Tech 5 Kirby and Panzeroberschütze Köhler were wounded within a day of one another, Kirby on February 21 and Köhler on the 22nd. All they know is that they were somewhere around Kasserine. Within days US morale improved as replacements and reinforcements arrived. Kirby recalls that word was spreading they thought they could stop the Germans and indeed, on February 22 Rommel began pulling back.

OVERLEAF
A victorious PzKpfw III passes a knocked-out and still burning M3 medium tank and M3 tank destroyer.

Its 50mm gun clearly visible, this PzKpfw III Ausf L served with the 6th Company, Panzer Regiment 7 of the 10th Panzer Division at Kasserine Pass.

Köhler recalls they were low on fuel and ammunition by that time. While there was concern about the Tigers, Kirby never saw one, but he heard that several had been knocked out by rear attack and fighter-bombers. The real duel was between M3s and Panzer IIIs and IVs.

Kirby thinks his tank was hit by a 75mm antitank gun on the left side. The driver was killed, and Kirby and his loader were sprayed by fragments, mostly in the legs. They experienced difficulties getting out, but the unwounded turret crew helped extract them. The tank caught fire as Kirby was carried to the rear. A serious knee injury saw Kirby being evacuated first to Britain by ship; the loader remained in Tunisia as far as he knows. After a month he sailed for the States where he was discharged before the year's end. He still limps from the injuries he sustained that day.

Köhler's unit was hit by artillery while moving to counterattack position to cover the withdrawal. He was atop the turret when five fragments struck him in the back, and he almost tumbled off the tank. An aid station was nearby, and he was driven to it. Köhler was placed on a litter, unloaded, and treated on the spot. He recalls that his tank went on into action and that the *Sanitäter* (medics) were keen on sending him to the rear before more casualties began coming in. The fragments were small but penetrated deeply, resulting in severe muscle damage. He lost his full range of right arm movement. About a week later he was flown to Sicily, shipped to Italy, and then to Germany by train for further surgery. Eventually he was assigned to a Panzer replacement training unit and instructed radio operators until the war's end.

STATISTICS AND ANALYSIS

It is difficult to say which of the two tanks, the M3 or the PzKpfw III, was the better one. The Germans had won the initial stages of the Kasserine battles through surprise and superior tactics, experience, solid command, and rapid decision making. In the end, however, the Americans regained the lost ground and forced the Germans to withdraw. The Americans had learned their lessons, and while tactical flexibility had contributed to this, it was mainly superior logistics with plentiful fuel, ammunition, supplies, and replacement vehicles and troops that enabled them to force the withdrawal. The M3 and PzKpfw III each had their own distinct advantages, capabilities, and limitations in armament, armor, mobility, reliability, and design. What it really came down to was the skills of the crew and small unit commanders and who was the quickest.

The 1st Armored Division and other units suffered serious but not devastating losses. Replacement equipment and personnel allowed them to quickly rebuild. The survivors of the 2d and 3d Battalions, 1st Armored Regiment were consolidated into a provisional 23d Armored Battalion. A field artillery battalion and a self-propelled artillery battery had to be reequipped along with a reconnaissance and an engineer company. In all the 1st Armored Division lost 1,401 troops dead, missing, captured, and wounded. This was exclusive of the attached units' losses. Much of the 34th Infantry Division's 168th Infantry had to be rebuilt, having lost over 1,800 troops, mostly captured.

The Germans reported the capture of over 4,000 American, British, and French troops, 58 machine guns, 25 40mm AA guns, five British 25-pdr gun-howitzers, 13 mortars, 13 AA guns, two 75mm self-propelled howitzers, three 105mm self-propelled howitzers, three tanks, 61 armored vehicles (mostly halftracks), 161 trucks, 45 tons of ammunition, 100 cubic meters of fuel, and 115 cubic meters of lubricants.

The fact that only three tanks were captured is attributed to the fact the Germans' AP ammunition had an HE charge, which caused tanks to burn or explode. For this reason, two months after the Sidi Bou Zid battle, over 40 American tanks were found rusting on the plain northwest of the town. They were damaged to the point that the Germans did not attempt to recover them. In all the Americans lost 89 medium tanks and almost as many lights.

It is difficult to determine the numbers of troops involved because the action was spread over a wide geographic area and one can use several different criteria for determining which units participated. Estimates claim that there were roughly 30,000 Allied and 22,000 Axis troops involved. There were some 10,000 Allied casualties, of which 6,500 were Americans, and 2,000 Axis casualties. The Americans lost 183 tanks and the Axis 34.

A knocked-out German Panzer
III with a dead crewman,
1943. (IWM NA 836)

AFTERMATH

The battles of Kasserine Pass were a sobering episode for the US Army. Even though the Americans had been ashore in North Africa for almost three months and had seen action, they were ill prepared to face the veteran Germans. In the rush to deploy the 1st Armored Division, it had not undertaken desert warfare training. American doctrine, tactics, and techniques at the time were guilty of unrealistic expectations with inadequate preparation. The doctrine was basically sound, but American leadership was too comfortable with its staged exercises in the large prewar and early war maneuvers. They were unprepared for the speed of events, the confusion, the loss of contact between units, and nonlinear dispositions. Additionally, the Americans did not have the skills to make the necessary immediate decisions without time for staff assessment and planning and then to implement them without hesitation. American reaction was often tardy, and a great deal of improvisation became necessary. The British raised a great outcry that the Americans were inexperienced and undertrained, but they too had paid dearly for their own experience.

The initial American defenses were haphazardly disposed, and units were splintered between commands, for example the 34th Infantry Division battalions being attached to the 1st Armored Division. It was discovered that the armored division was deficient in infantry, requiring its attachment from infantry divisions. Nonmotorized infantry were of limited use and suited only for holding terrain, if the terrain was tankproof. Infantry marching cross-country could not keep pace with faster moving armor, and nonmotorized units were at the mercy of a more mobile enemy. Mine detection and clearance capabilities were seriously wanting, and the Americans had to learn to lay mines effectively and rapidly when preparing a defense. The Germans surprised American counterattacks by the seemingly immediate appearance of minefields. Allied air support was dismal and poorly coordinated.

Fighter-bomber strikes were often too late to have any effect and the Axis virtually owned the sky.

Later in the action the Americans were able to establish more resolute defenses and often made good use of the terrain to hamper Panzers. Tank destroyer and reconnaissance units were employed for screening and secured flanks. It was found that light tanks offered little combat power and were suitable only for reconnaissance and screening. Pure light tank battalions would soon disappear as would regimental reconnaissance companies, and each medium battalion received a light company. M3 light tanks would be phased out and replaced by M5A1s, and of course the M3 medium was soon replaced by the M4.

The M3 medium tank, while providing a lethal 75mm gun and reasonable mechanical reliability, otherwise performed marginally for reasons discussed previously. The M4 was proved a more effective tank, but its propensity for catching fire was recognized. One AFV that did perform well was the 105mm M7 self-propelled howitzer on an M3 chassis. A major problem was encountered with the American 75mm AP ammunition, which lacked an explosive charge at this time. It may have penetrated most German tanks, but lacking a burster charge it caused fewer casualties, inflicted less interior damage, and seldom caused a fire. This allowed a large numbers of German tanks to be recovered, repaired, and returned to service.

Tunisia 1943: American M3 tank churning through thick mud during the North African campaign. (Getty)

The Germans, because of their fewer number of tanks, often maintained only a very small reserve, that is, *"Alles in die Waagschale werfen"* ("to throw everything into the scale pan"). On the other hand they were familiar with the US practice of deploying two subunits forward and retaining one in support or reserve – two up, one back – a tank battalion deploying two companies forward and one in reserve, for example. To counter this the Germans would execute a double envelopment to cut off the support. The Germans were also adept at luring American tanks, which tended to maintain a cavalry charge mentality, into traps where they were engaged by waiting Panzers and antitank guns. The 8.8cm Flak, while an antiaircraft gun, was often used to engage tanks and could knock out any Allied tank even at its maximum range. Another surprise for the Americans was that the Germans were just as likely to attack at dusk as at dawn, the former being unexpected. The Germans were also noted for their rapid decision making and taking immediate advantage of emerging situations. However, they sometimes hesitated to pursue withdrawing American units, perhaps feeling they might be drawn into ambush along the line of their own tactics. Moreover, they became increasingly cautious as their tank strength dwindled.

Even with the obvious faults of the M3 medium, the light tanks, and halftracks, the Germans were astounded by the quality and quantity of American weapons, equipment, and supplies. They welcomed the captured fuel and excellent rations, but they were concerned with the quality of the weapons and vehicles. They understood the Americans were inexperienced and unfamiliar with the desert, but they foresaw a tough, well-armed opponent in the future.

In his autobiography, Panzer Commander Oberst Hans von Luck stated, "We admired the courage and élan with which the Americans executed their attacks, even though we sometimes felt sorry for them at having to pay for the combat experience with such heavy losses. We discovered later, in Italy, and I personally in the battles in France in 1944, how quickly the Americans were able to evaluate their experience and, through flexible and unconventional conduct of a battle, convert it into results."

Rommel supported von Luck's assessment. "Although it is true the American troops could not yet be compared with the veteran troops of the Eighth Army, yet they made up for their lack of experience by their far better and more plentiful equipment and their tactically more flexible command. In fact, their armament in antitank weapons and armored vehicles was so enormous that we could look forward with all but small hope of success to the coming mobile battles."

The major defeat of American forces at Kasserine was the last victory the Germans experienced in North Africa. Having spent much of their armor and resources and suffering the increasing Allied successes in interdicting Axis resupply efforts across the Mediterranean, the Germans and Italians were gradually compressed into northern Tunisia. Hitler's wish that there would be no "German Dunkirk" was obeyed and they surrendered on May 12, 1943. A final message was transmitted: "In accordance with orders received Afrikakorps has fought itself to the condition where it can fight no more."

BIBLIOGRAPHY AND FURTHER READING

Armored Replacement Training Center. "Tankers in Tunisia." Ft Knox, KY: US
    Army (1943) Available on-line
    http://www.lonesentry.com/manuals/tankers/tankers_pp_preface.html.
Atkinson, Rick, *An Army at Dawn: The War in Africa, 1942–1943*, New York:
    Henry Holt (2002)
Baily, Charles M., *Faint Praise: American Tanks and Tank Destroyers During World
    War II*, Hamden, PA: Archon Books (1983)
Bender, James, and Warren W. Odegard, *Uniforms, Organization and History of the
    Panzertruppe*, San Jose, CA: R. James Bender Publishing (1980)
Blumenson, Martin, *Kasserine Pass: Rommel's Bloody, Climactic Battle for Tunisia*,
    New York: Houghton Mifflin (1966)
Ellis, Chris, and Hilary Doyle, *Panzerkampfwagen: German Combat Tanks 1933–
    1945*, Auburn, CA: Argus Books (1976)
Gudgin, Peter, *Armoured Firepower: The Development of Tank Armament 1939–45*,
    Gloucestershire: Sutton Publishing (1997)
Hart, B.H. Liddell, *The Rommel Papers*, New York: Harcourt, Brace and Company
    (1953)
Howe, George F., *Northwest Africa: Seizing the Initiative in the West. US Army in
    World War II*, Washington, DC: Office of the Chief of Military History (1957)
    ———. *The Battle History of the 1st Armored Division*, Washington, DC: Combat

Forces Press (1954)

Hunnicutt, R.P., *Sherman: A History of the American Medium Tank,* Novato, CA: Presidio Press (1978)

Jentz, Thomas J., *Tank Combat in North Africa: The Opening Rounds,* Atglen, PA: Schiffer Military History (1998)

Kelly, Orr, *Meeting the Fox: The Allied Invasion of Africa, from Operation Torch to Kasserine Pass to Victory in Tunisia,* Indianapolis, IN: Wiley Publishing (2002)

Rolf, David, *The Bloody Road to Tunis,* London: Greenhill (2001)

Schneider, Wolfgang, *Panzer Tactics: German Small-Unit Armor Tactics in World War II,* Mechanicsburg, PA: Stackpole Books (2005)

Sharp, Charles C., *German Panzer Tactics in World War II,* West Chester, OH: George F. Nafziger (1998)

von Luck, Hans, *Panzer Commander,* Westport, CT: Praeger Publishers (1989)

Watson, Bruce, *Exit Rommel: The Tunisian Campaign 1942–43,* Westport, CT: Praeger Publishers (1999)

INDEX

Figures in **bold** refer to illustrations.

Ambrosio, Gen 29
ambush, armor (*Panzerwarte*) **46**
armament, M3
  gun, 37mm M5 **9**, 12, 31
  gun, 37mm M6 12, 31, 32–33
  gun, 75mm M2 1112, 31, 32, 34–35
  gun, 75mm M3 11–12, 31, 32, 34–35
  cleaning **51**
  machine gun, .30cal **9**, 11, **41**
armament, PzKpfw III
  gun, 3.7cm KwK 36 L/45 20, 40
  gun, 5cm KwK 37 L/60 40
  gun, 5cm KwK 38 L/42 20, 40
  gun, 5cm KwK 39 L/60 20
  gun, 7.5cm KwK 37 L/24 20
Arnim, Gen der Panzertruppen Hans-Jürgen von 27, 29

British Army
  Armoured Division, 6th 27
  Army, Eighth 6, 24, 25, 27, 28
  Corps, V 27
British Tank Commission 36

Chrysler Motors Corporation 9, 10, **13**, 14
Commonwealth Western Desert Force 22, 24
Cramer, Genlt Hans 27

Daimler–Benz 17
  Typ ZW40 tank **6**
Das Reich 35
design and development
  M3 medium tank 8–15
  PzKpfw III light tank 16–18, 20–21
Detroit Tank Arsenal 9, 10, **13**
Djebel Ksaira 29, 30, 57, 62, 66
Djebel Lessouda 29, 30, 61, 62

Eastern Dorsal Mountains 28, 29
Eisenhower, Gen Dwight D. 25, 29, 57
El Alamein, Battle of (1942) 6, 26, 30
El Guettar, battle of (1943) 28

Faïd Pass 27, 28, 29, 30, 60
French Corps, XIX 27

Gazala Line, battle of (1942) 6, 24, 25
German army
  Deutsches Afrikakorps 24, 25, 28, 50
  Division von Broich 27
  Heereswaffenamt (Army Weapons Office) 16
  Infanterie Division, 334.: 27
  Kampfgruppe Gerhardt 30, 61
  Kampfgruppe Lang 30
  Kampfgruppe Reimann 30, 61
  Kampfgruppe Schuette 30, 61–62
  Kampfgruppe Stenkhoff 30, 62, 64
  Korpsgruppe Fischer 27
  leichte Afrika–Division, 90.: 24
  leichte Panzer-Division, 5. (later 21. Panzer Division) 22, 24
  Panzer-Armee, 5.: 27, 29
  Panzer-Division, 7.: 59
  Panzer-Division, 10. 7, 27, 30, 48, 50, 58, 60, 64–66, 67, 69
  Panzer-Division, 15. 7, 24, 27, 50
  Panzer-Division, 21. (formerly 5. leichte Division) 7, 24, 27, 28, 30, 50, 58, 60, 61, 64, 67, 69
  Panzer-Regiment 7: 18, 64–66, **72**
  Panzertruppe insignia **59**
  Panzertruppenschule 44
  Panzerwaffe 44, 45

Halfaya Pass 24
Henry, Sergeant 67, 68
Hitler, Adolf 26, 77

intelligence, Enigma 30
Italian forces 22
  XX, XXI and XXX Corpo 27

Kasserine Pass 7, **28**, 28, 29, 69
Kern's Crossroads 64
"Kirby, Tech 5 Paul" 63, 67, 68–69, 72
Köhler, Panzeroberschütze Baldur 59, 64–66, 69, 72

Luck, Obst Hans von 77

M2 tank 5, **8**, 8, 9
M2A1 medium tank 9, 10
M3 medium tank 24, **32**, **33**, **41**, **69**, 76 *see also* design and development, M3 medium tank; specifications, technical, M3
  ammunition 13, **14**, 34, 52 *see also* armament, M3
  communications 43–44
  crew **14**, **41**, **48**, **51**, **52**, **54**
  engine 13, 14
  flaws 33–34, 35
  front views **9**, **11**
  Grant **12**, 36–37
    driver's compartment **56**
  layout 11–13
  Lee **12**, 35, **36**, 36–37
  overhead view **7**
  production 15
  rear view **11**
  side view **10**
  support roles 37
  turret **34**
  variants 13–15
    M3A1 **12**, 13, 14, 31
    M3A2 13, 14, 31
    M3A3 **12**, 14, 31
    M3A4 14–15, 31
    M3A5 **10**, **13**, 14, 31
M4 (T6) *Sherman* medium tank 10, 34, 26, 76
Malta 22, 25
Mareth Line 27, 28, 29
Medjez el Bab 7
Montgomery, Gen Bernard 25, 26
Mussolini, Benito 22, 29

National Defense Advisory Board 36
National Socialist Motorized Corps (NSKK) 45

Operation
  Frülingswind (Spring Wind) 29, 30
  Kuckuchsei (Cuckoo's Egg) 29
  Morgenluft (Morning Breeze) 29
  Torch 6, 25, 26, 34
organization, unit
  German 50–51
  US Army 49–50

Patton, Lt Gen George **26**
PzKfz III tank 9, 10, 11
PzKfz IV tank 9–10
PzKpfw (Panzer) I light tank 16
PzKpfw II light tank 16
PzKpfw III light tank 25, 27, **69**, **74** *see also* design and development, PzKpfw III
  ammunition **19**, 21 *see also* armament, PzKpfw III
  captured **6**
  command vehicle 44
  communications 46–48
  crew **43**, **45**, **49**
  engine 20
  front view **19**
  gunner's view 66–67
  layout 18, 20–21
  manufacturers 20
  production 20
  rear view **19**
  side view **18**
  support roles 40
  turret **38**
  variants 20
    PzKpfw III Ausf A **16**, 17, 20
    PzKpfw III Ausf B/C/D/E/F 20
    PzKpfw III Ausf J 20, 38, 39
    PzKpfw III Ausf J: loader's position **40**

PzKpfw III Ausf L **37**, **72** *see also* specifications, technical, PzKpfw III Ausf L
PzKpfw III Ausf L(tp) (*tropisch*) 39
PzKpfw III Ausf M 18
PzKpfw III Ausf N 20, **61**
PzKpfw IV medium tank 16–17, 40
PzKpfw IV Ausf H medium tank 20–21
PzKpfw V Tiger tank 7, 58

Rebaou Pass 28, 29
Rock Island Arsenal 9
Rommel, GFM Erwin 6, 7, **22**, 22, 24–25, 26, 27, 29, 37, 69, 77

Sbeïtla, defense of (1943) **62**, 67–69, 72
Sidi Bou Zid 29, 30, 57, **60**
  battle of (1943) **58**, **60**, 60–62, 64–67
signals, hand smoke (*Handrauchzeichen*) 46
specifications, technical, M3 31–35
  in Commonwealth service 35, 36–37
  Lee 35, 36–37
specifications, technical, PzKpfw III Ausf L 38–40
statistics 73–74
strategic situation 22, 24–30
  February 1943 22, **23**, 24
  new front in northwest Africa 26–27
  tactical situation 28–30
Stumme, Gen 25, 26

T5 medium tank, projected 8–9
tank destroyer, M3 **69**
tankers' daily life 51–56
  ammunition, restocking 52
  in combat 55–56 *see also* "Kirby, Tech 5 Paul"; Köhler, Panzeroberschütze Baldur
  conditions in tank 53
  rations 53–54
  sleeping arrangements 54–55
  stimulants 55
tankers' duties, German 45–48, 56
tankers' duties, US Army 43–44, 56
tanks, American, nicknaming 15
Task Force Kern 29, 57
Task Force Stark 29
terrain 29–30
Tobruk 24, 25, 26
training, German 44–45
training, US Army 41–43, **42**
Tripoli 22
Tunis 28
Tunisia 26–27, 28–30

US Army
  Armor School, Ft Knox 42
  Armored Division, 1st 7, **24**, 28, 42, 58, 62, 73, 75
    Combat Command A (CCA) 27, 29, 61, 62, 64
    Combat Command B (CCB) 27, 49, 67
    Combat Command C (CCC) 27, 29, 57
    Combat Command D (CCD) 27, 29
  Armored Field Artillery Bn, 27th 67
  Armored Force 42
    insignia **63**
  Armored Infantry, 6th, 1st Bn 64
  Armored Infantry, 6th, 2d Bn 67
  Armored Regiment, 1st, 3d Bn 57, 61, 62
  Armored Regiment, 13th, 2d Bn **11**, **24**, 32, 49, 63, 67, 68–69
  Corps, II 7, 27
  Infantry Brigade, 139th 27
  Infantry Division, 1st 27
  Infantry Division, 34th 27, 73, 75
  Ordnance Committee 8
  Ordnance Department 10
  Tank Battalion, 751st 49
  Tank Destroyer Bn, 601st 67

Ziegler, Gen 64